GARDEN STYLE

Better Homes and Gardens® Books
Des Moines, Iowa

Better Homes and Gardens® Books
An imprint of Meredith® Books

Garden Style

Editor: Linda Hallam

Contributing Editors: Mary Baskin, Kristine Carber, Nancy Ingram, Heather Lobdell, Elaine Markoutsas, Elle Roper, Tangi Schaapveld

Senior Associate Design Director: Richard Michels

Illustrator: Brian Cronin

Stylist: Wade Scherrer

Copy Chief: Catherine Hamrick

Copy and Production Editor: Terri Fredrickson

Contributing Copy Editor: Kathleen Richardson

Contributing Proofreaders: Becky Danley, Diane Doro, Beth Lastine

Indexer: Kathleen Poole

Electronic Production Coordinator: Paula Forest

Editorial and Design Assistants: Kaye Chabot, Judy Bailey, Treesa Landry, Karen Schirm

Production Director: Douglas M. Johnston

Production Manager: Pam Kvitne

Assistant Prepress Manager: Marjorie J. Schenkelberg

Meredith® Books

Editor in Chief: James D. Blume

Design Director: Matt Strelecki

Managing Editor: Gregory H. Kayko

Executive Shelter Editor: Denise L. Caringer

Director, Sales & Marketing, Retail: Michael A. Peterson

Director, Sales & Marketing, Special Markets: Rita McMullen

Director, Sales & Marketing, Home & Garden Center Channel: Ray Wolf

Director, Operations: George A. Susral

Vice President, General Manager: Jamie L. Martin

Better Homes and Gardens® Magazine

Editor in Chief: Jean LemMon

Executive Interior Design Editor: Sandra S. Soria

Meredith Publishing Group

President, Publishing Group: Christopher M. Little

Vice President, Consumer Marketing & Development: Hal Oringer

Meredith Corporation

Chairman and Chief Executive Officer: William T. Kerr

Chairman of the Executive Committee: E. T. Meredith III

Cover Photograph: Jenifer Jordan.

2

Creating Garden Style

I grew up in South Louisiana, where the lines between indoors and out are as nebulous as the seasons. Live oaks draped with legendary Spanish moss are green all winter, and striped camellias bloom at Christmas. I live now in a place with four distinct seasons and snow that blankets our gardens in winter. But I've found that when I decorate my home with plants and gently aged garden furniture, outdoor ornaments, and tools, when I bring the outdoors inside, I enjoy the warmth of summer throughout the year. In this, I emulate Elvin McDonald, a garden writer, whose home, filled with blooming plants and garden ornaments on a cold winter day, inspired this book. And the credit goes, too, to all the gardeners, garden style decorators, and shop owners who have opened their homes, gardens, shops, and ideas to me. Across the country, from large cities to small towns, they create garden style as a lifestyle that erases any boundaries between indoors and outdoors. Garden style is their way to decorate, live, and entertain with the warmth, beauty, and simplicity of nature. I thank them all for sharing their love of the garden and garden style.   —Linda Hallam, Editor, *Garden Style*

Table Of Contents

INSPIRED By The GARDEN

Creating FRESH-AIR ROOMS

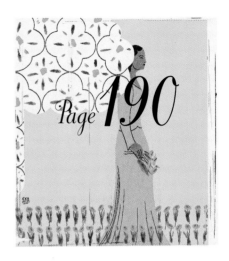

Page 54

Page 135

Page 190

BRINGING
The
OUTDOORS
In

LIVING
The
GARDEN
Life

IDEAS
SOURCES,
Inspirations

INSPIRED
By The
GARDEN

ardening satisfies our cravings for fresh air and sunshine. Gardening soothes our souls and replenishes our spirits. When we garden, we learn to appreciate the rhythms of the seasons and the patience to wait for spring flowers to bloom, for summer vegetables to ripen on

their vines. Now much more than a hobby, gardening is an avocation, a way of life that returns us to the serenity of nurturing life from the soil. We long to keep the garden with us, indeed around us, whether we dine outdoors under an arbor, dripping with vines, or warm our winter-chilled homes with leafy green plants, fresh flowers, and timeworn tools and furnishings. With the garden as inspiration, we erase the boundaries between outdoors and indoors, between the seasons. With every page of *Better Homes and Gardens® Garden Style*, the garden becomes a means of expression, not just a backdrop to our lifestyle. The garden inspires not just how we decorate our home, but how we live and entertain our friends.

Garden-style decorating is as individual as every person, and it can start with one special element. Picture in your mind what you love about the outdoors, the garden, and what appeals to you. Nothing has to be expensive or costly to decorate in garden style. Some of the most charming rooms and outdoor settings are created from castoffs and found objects. If you like an old urn, a metal gate, an architectural fragment, or a vintage bench from the garden, bring it inside. Gently aged elements from the garden look even more charming when you mix them with floral fabrics, botanical prints, vintage pottery, and pretty, fresh colors. The mix of elements and the pairing of old and new are the relaxed charm of the garden.

Garden-style decorating speaks to what you cherish, to what is meaningful to you. If you value your mother's old garden tools or watering cans or similar objects of sentiment you've found in your rounds of flea markets and garage sales, bring them inside. It's refreshing and reassuring to think that objects are valued for their sentiments, memories, meanings to our lives and families rather than for their lengthy pedigrees or costly price tags. New and reproduction ornaments—folk art for the garden you've found on a trip, a beautiful birdbath, or sundial from a shop you're discovered—have their own meaning to your life and your garden style.

The beauty of garden-style decorating is that it works anywhere, any time, in any climate

Why not set *a table* and serve summer dinners on *the porch* or deck at sunset?

from the smallest city apartment to the grandest country home. When the peace and joys of the garden are welcome, you'll always feel at ease and at home. And you'll enjoy warmth and greenery on the coldest of winter days.

Whether you are an avid garden-style decorator or just discovering the style, you'll be

8

motivated by "Creating Fresh-Air Rooms," beginning on page 14. As you look through this chapter, you'll want to decorate your outdoor spaces with the comforts of your indoor rooms. Think about chairs and ottomans that are truly comfortable

too, for ideas on linens, accessories, and tools that make your fresh-air spaces all the more welcoming for casual entertaining.

And when your finds and treasures begin to migrate inside your home, turn to "Bringing the Outdoors In," on page 52. From living

Some of the *most charming* rooms are created from *castoffs* and found objects.

and would be even more welcoming with soft cushions and pillows. Remember, too, how handy small tables are inside for drinks and books and place them at strategic spots on your porch or deck or in your outdoor room. Look through this chapter,

rooms and kitchens to the nursery, every room of your home relaxes with the elements and motifs of the outdoors. Simple touches such as a kitchen window filled with plants or flowers from your garden make a difference in how your home feels. You'll see how the elements

of the garden—and garden-inspired fabrics and decorative elements—can fill your home with the warmth, beauty, and ease of the outdoors. For ideas and inspiration from experienced garden-style decorators,

climate, they all illustrate the beauty of indoor and outdoor designs in harmony with nature. When you are looking for sources for garden style decorating, you'll find photographs and decorating ideas from trendsetting shops and

the beauty of *garden-style* decorating is that it works *anywhere,* in any climate

tour the five homes and their gardens in "Living the Garden Life," starting on page 128. From Connecticut to California, they open their doors and garden gates and share their thoughtful ideas on indoor and outdoor decorating. Though each home is different and each responds to the region and

the addresses of many more across the country, beginning on page 180. Many of the shops are noted for display ideas as you'll see and are destinations for travelers and as well as finds for neighborhood residents. Mail-order and national retail sources are listed as are antique shops with garden ornaments and furniture.

Creating
FRESH-AIR
ROOMS

cro
nin

arden style begins the easiest and most natural way, with the outdoors. For your own personal outdoor room, start with what suits you, your home and garden, and your climate. Like interior spaces, fresh-air rooms can be elaborately planned and detailed, or charming

in their simplicity. Formal symmetrical planting beds, with paths and a roofed dining pavilion, may be your dream of an outdoor living room. Or a pair of backyard Adirondack chairs sharing a small, metal bistro table for drinks and books—or even a hammock between two shade trees—could be the right touches for how you enjoy outdoor living and relaxing.

Rethinking how you use your garden or porch may be all it takes to create a comfortable, inviting outdoor living room. For dining and sitting, add a gravel terrace for an outdoor dining room, or shade a patio table and chairs with a sturdy canvas umbrella.

As with indoor decorating, details and finishing touches translate into inviting, personal

spaces. Even if your outdoor room is as simple as Adirondack chairs and table, decorate it with plant-filled terra-cotta pots on stands. When friends drop by for lemonade, dress up your outdoor room with colorful accent pillows and drape the table with a cotton cloth.

Garden ornaments, too, are always welcome for color and personality in outdoor rooms of any size or style. Bring out your watering cans or outdoor lanterns; find places for cast-concrete finials or decorative birdbaths. When you decorate outdoors, you decorate for the occasion, for the season. Let fresh-air decorating be as fun and evolving as your passions. The fresh-air rooms you create can be your own movable feast. Enjoy them.

Living On The Porch

long the Alabama Gulf Coast, the porches of old bayside houses were built to capture the cooling breezes. This new bay house gracefully emulates the historic style with a full-length 15 x 80-foot screened porch for living, dining, and entertaining. In the tradition of the neighboring 19th-century summer homes, pairs of French doors open the interior spaces to this shady retreat. Shutters protect the west side from the burning afternoon sun. A casual mix of cushioned rockers, chairs, and tables furnishes the open-air living room.

collect *comfortable* furnishings

Vintage and reproduction furniture and accessories mix easily
to transform this bayside screened porch into an inviting
living and dining room. The secret to unifying? White paint,
blue and white stripes, and white cloths for dining. Colorful
hydrangea and white gardenias recall old Southern gardens.

enliven *with* blue and white

Think classic color combinations, such as blue and white, for porch furniture. Rocking chairs work with a variety of styles; give yours an updated look with white enamel. Small tables from thrift stores and wicker trunks are equally versatile and add storage for coasters, magazines, or even table linens.

Porch
Pleasures

ront porches invite the neighbors to walk up and chat. Side porches encourage reading, talking, relaxing. Back porches bring the garden inside. Whatever your house and setting, there are few things more fun than a swing, a glass of lemonade, and a long, lazy afternoon on the porch. Porches are back in vogue for both remodeling and new construction as families look for ways to create casual fresh-air rooms and retreats. If you have one, enjoy your haven with comfortable furnishings, a ceiling fan, and plants. If you don't, a porch addition may be the remodeling you need to bring garden style into your home.

enjoy *your* vintage wicker

For porch furniture that never dates, shop for restored and reproduction white wicker in comfortable shapes and sizes. A mix of fabric patterns, plants, and accessories easily changes with the season and occasion.

energize *with a* patterned rug

For funky fun, mix a colorful, durable kilim or dhurrie rug
with oversized twig and smaller-scale dining furniture. Add
your favorite outdoor touches, such as the porch bracket and
wire plant stand, for your take on lighthearted garden style.

When you entertain fresh-air style, collect
linens in color combinations that are easy to mix
and match. Blue and white is a crisp, classic
combination that never goes out of style and
works with red or yellow and touches of green.

accenting *with* red touches

installing *window* boxes

Enjoy happy color with seasonal plantings in
window boxes, pots, or hanging baskets.
Here, the overflowing mix of flowers and vines
dresses a rustic porch, furnished with always
classic white wicker pieces and plump cushions.

Vintage wicker pieces retain their value when
the original finish is gently restored, not
repainted. If you find old pieces, such as these
with light and dark finishes, feel free to mix
fabrics to tie your scheme together.

the romance of *wicker and* florals

old glory *colors* for summer

Enjoy a sporty, all-American look with red and
blue accents in a patriotic scheme. Choose
family-friendly pieces—such as the classic painted
Adirondack chairs with ottoman, bench, and rope
hammock—that stand up to everyday living.

tailored *neutral* stripes

*For a sophisticated dining porch, hang draperies
that fold back gracefully to reveal the scene.
Heavy, lined cottons work for year-round use
on a covered porch. Or drape lightweight
cottons or sheers if you decorate for the season.*

pair a swing *with* rockers

Take advantage of your screened porch by
starting with the basics—a porch swing and
sturdy rockers with woven seats. Add
familiar living room touches, such as a braided
rag rug and tables for drinks and flowers.

waking to *a lake* view

In this lodgelike setting, a cot suspended by strong chains lulls its occupant to sleep. Perfect for cool summer nights, the setting also invites lazy afternoons of reading and napping. Red, white, and blue bedding recalls summer camps.

candles *for* soft lighting

Turn down the tempo of your life with an open-air room that includes wall-mounted sconces for the glow of evening candlelight. Neutral colors and cool greens enhance the quiet setting designed for end-of-the-day serenity.

paint *flowers* overhead

Why not take advantage of the charm of a bead-board ceiling with an overhead garden of painted blossoms or colorful leaves? Choose a pretty color, such as this yellow, or the pale green or blue used traditionally for porch ceilings.

Terraces & Outdoor Rooms

utdoor rooms without roofs, inviting terraces, patios, and courtyards take advantage of sun and views. Combined with porches or decks, these open spaces expand your home and garden with sunny additions and possibilities for under-the-stars entertaining and dining. Often included in new construction, patios and decks adapt to most house styles and lots. Patios, a suburban staple for decades, open houses to the backyard and the outdoors. When shade is a necessity because of a sunny orientation, arbors, trellises, and fixed or retractable awnings decoratively protect from the heat of a summer day.

well-furnished *outdoor* rooms

If you leave removable cushions outside during warm weather, look for ones made for outdoor use—or check with a fabric store about laminating a sturdy cotton for longer wear. Include pillows to brighten the look and wire plant stands that easily can be replenished with the season.

Emulate the romance of the woods on your
terrace with twig furniture and colorful pillows
and cushions. Look for new twig furniture in
shops that carry regional crafts or older pieces
in antique shops and vintage furniture stores.

rustic *appeal* of twig

quick color *with* tablecloths

Turn your terrace into an outdoor dining room
with a bistro or ice cream parlor metal table
and chairs. With such quaint pieces, you need
only a cheerful cotton cloth and a fresh-fruit
centerpiece to welcome guests with style.

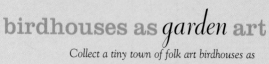

birdhouses as garden art

Collect a tiny town of folk art birdhouses as
a focal point for your garden. When you dine
alfresco, dress a picnic-style or rustic farm
table with pretty shawls. Instead of the expected
benches, group with worn bistro chairs.

paint your garden gate blue

Perk up a garden or a courtyard with one
cheerful color. For a touch of Provence, choose
a French blue or rusty red as your accent.
Shop for table linens in solids, stripes, or florals
that pair with your bright accent.

The Terrace As Skyline Garden

iews of the Chicago skyline unfold as a dramatic backdrop for this urban oasis on the fourth level of a graystone townhouse. Lush plantings enrich the rooftop retreat for country garden appeal. In this tucked-away secret garden, the enchantment leads from the master bedroom through the Victorian screen door, under a pergola dripping with scarlet runner beans, to a small patio filled with container plants. Beyond the gate, with a window box, and under another pergola is the rest of the garden—and the city. Wooden barrels planted with sunflowers, cosmos, and vegetables pack the rooftop.

frame the city view

More than a terrace with a view, this rooftop flower and vegetable garden creates country in the city with a picket fence and a latched gate with its own planter box. The structural wood is simple pressure-treated pine, left unfinished to weather naturally to soft shades of gray.

Warmed By The Fire

When you enjoy outdoor living, extend your pleasure months longer with an outdoor fireplace on your terrace, porch, or loggia. In cool climates, outdoor fireplaces warm spring or fall nights too nippy for comfortable sitting or dining. And in warm climates, where fireplaces are rarely needed, the romance of fireside dining can be yours on starry late fall or clear winter nights. Portable fireplaces in a variety of price ranges are available for warmth without a building commitment. See page 215 for shops and mail-order sources.

elements of *the French* garden

Emulate the comfort- and style-loving French with a
porch designed for relaxing and entertaining. Include
armchairs with cushions and a table for drinks and snacks.
A barrel brimming with tools, a tree-trunk garden stool,
and a stylized birdcage enliven with fanciful touches.

Decks For Entertaining

On the first warm night of spring, ready your deck for a casual dinner with a colorful tablecloth, cushions for the chairs, pots of blooming flowers, and candlelight. Whatever the size, shape, or configuration, decks offer the potential for inviting fresh-air rooms with the elements and motifs of the garden. When you entertain, fill watering cans or flower buckets with garden flowers. And convert a child's metal wagon or wheelbarrow into a rolling cart for iced-down beverages. Even a practical potting bench doubles as a server for snacks or buffet suppers.

planters *enrich* color

Think of a plain deck as backdrop, and collect pots and planters in a variety of sizes, shapes, colors, and materials. Plant with shrubs, perennials, and annuals appropriate to your climate and sun exposure. Incorporate trellises or elevate some planters on stands for height.

flowers in elevated pots

Brighten a small deck with easy-to-plant
and replant pots of blooming flowers.
Elevate and hang terra-cotta pots for interest.
In this flowery mood, mix patterns of
floral cushions and pillows for seating comfort.

structure *for* shade

Enjoy a large deck even more with a shady, wisteria-covered arbor and an old-fashioned porch swing. Here, lush pots of mixed flowers and climbing roses turn the deck into a verdant garden retreat for relaxing and entertaining.

Potting Sheds

Designed as playhouses for gardeners, potting sheds combine the practical with the aesthetic. Such structures offer places to pot, plant, prune, and nurture your plants—and serve as the focal points of gardens. These little houses can be as simple or as elaborate as your interests, climate, and budget dictate. Inside, the plants, tools, and pots are practical reminders of the garden outside. Depending on your needs and space, include lights, heat, or water. For lovers of garden style, these quaint hideaways lend themselves to casual retreats for meditating, sitting, dining, or entertaining like-minded souls.

GARDEN HERBS

recycle *flea* market finds

To organize your potting shed,
shop flea markets and
secondhand stores for sturdy
work tables, gently worn chairs,
boxes, and containers.
Use the wall to hang tools and
charts, both old and new, and
add a drying rack to preserve
the fruits of your labors.

Painted plywood shelves and a skirted
built-in counter turn a tiny nook into a potting
area perfect for arranging flowers and
reviving houseplants. Utilitarian under-the-
counter storage is handy, yet out of sight.

tuck in space *to pot or* prune

organize with *rustic* baskets

If space and plumbing allow, a work counter
with a sink adds convenience to your potting
and flower-arranging area. Here, the counter,
backsplash, and shelf crafted from barn-type
wood enhance the country style.

entertain *in the garden shed*

With nods to the useful and the decorative,
this garden house welcomes workdays as well
as casual, open-air entertaining. The quirky
mix of chairs and furnishings reflects the owner's
love of vintage, country-style furniture.

Structure For The Garden

When the English designed structures of all shapes, sizes, and styles for their gardens, they called the more eccentric of them follies. In France, from the lavish days of the 18th century, structures in the garden were *petites maisons* (small houses). Variations of both have been built in the Americas since colonial days—as visual elements that are parts of garden plans and as protected spots for dining or sitting. American classics are open-air gazebos, scaled-down versions of those built in town squares, and vine-covered arbors. When space is tight, an arbor with a bench is a garden house for two.

If your retreat is a gazebo, re-create the pleasures of Victorian-era outdoor teas with a tablecloth, set table, and appropriately embellished teapot. Hanging ferns recall a much-beloved plant used in the 19th century.

tea time *in the* gazebo

greenhouse *as garden* house

Well-designed greenhouses provide protection for plants and a focus to the landscape. Here, a vine-covered, cottage-style greenhouse features recycled windows, replete with muntin bars for the roof, and casement windows for ventilation.

Inspired by the porch swing, this bungalow's screened porch relaxes for warm weather with a sisal rug and furnishings from import stores and catalogs. Touches of green update with bright color.

before:

Dressed For Summer Living

Think of your porch as a room, and you'll be inspired by the fun of quick decorating. Here, the lack of privacy on a city lot and the western exposure deterred the owner from enjoying the screened porch. As a solution, she sewed sheer cotton panels to gather on standard tension rods that fit inside the screen frames. Import-store glass urns support a stock glass tabletop for the coffee table. Torch-style, glass-globe candleholders in a metal flower bucket and a retro-look electric fan on a woven table add summery finishing touches. As an alternative to glass urns, substitute large terra-cotta pots or cast concrete urns. And instead of a swing, try a rope hammock, a pair of painted porch rockers, metal garden chairs, or wicker or rattan armchairs for convivial groupings.

the makeover:

Furnishings and quick-and-easy window treatments transform a bleak porch into this warm-weather family room. An inexpensive birdbath doubles as a table for magazines.

before:

50

Style &
The Three-
Season Porch

aximize the potential of this suburban staple by creating a true garden living room that's comfortable much of the year. As a first step, assess how you plan to use the space. Here, the family wanted a living area that would work as a potting shed/greenhouse. To give the porch a real-room feel, fluttery, unlined, hemmed muslin squares, hung pennantlike from bamboo rods, soften the screens, and a sisal rug covers the decking. (If sun control is an issue, substitute roll-up bamboo blinds.) A pair of wicker armchairs and a wicker lounge chair with an ottoman invite guests to linger. Thrift-store tables are handy for books and drinks, and a rustic table organizes houseplants. Wall-hung frosted glass vases add a refined balance to plants in baskets and pots.

BRINGING The OUTDOORS In

The pleasure of garden style is that no matter where you live, no matter the season, you can invite the outdoors into your home. Houseplants; flower-filled pottery vases; vintage garden accessories and tools; and simple, timeworn furniture are equally at home in a city apartment,

a house in the suburbs, or a country cottage. By degrees, gardeners and garden-style decorators are erasing the lines between furnishings and accessories for our homes and gardens. Urns, ivy topiaries, and terra-cotta pots find welcome as they relax formal, traditional rooms or warm sleek, contemporary settings.

As garden style becomes your own look, you'll gravitate to the soft colors and botanical patterns of nature. Consider tints of fresh green or hints of warm yellow for the backdrops to the fragments and outdoor elements that are hallmarks of bringing the outdoors in.

Think about which of your rooms most reflects the garden and the joys of the outdoors. Even a few little touches—antique hand tools on a shelf or table, fern prints on the wall, an iron patio table for plants, books, or magazines—speak of your love for gardening and the outdoors. If your family room or breakfast nook opens to a deck or porch, garden elements, such as an aged stepladder for plants, outdoor tables, or folding bistro chairs, naturally find their way inside. If you enjoy indoor gardening, turn a corner of your kitchen into a potting area, with tools and containers as part of the decor.

Or decorate your nursery or child's room with the charm and whimsy of a lamp made from a watering can and a painted porch rocker with floral cushions for sturdy seating. In this easy style, finding decorative uses for such everyday objects is part of the fun.

Living In The Garden

hen you love garden style, live with a relaxed look that's fun to change with your current interests and newest finds. Do you like old iron gates, picket fences, garden benches? Rooms that open wide with sleek garden furniture and oversized planters? Or the charm of distressed furniture and vintage botanical prints? With carefully chosen elements, your garden style translates into your decorating style. When the style is new to you, start where you feel most comfortable. Accessories, such as small urns or garden-motif pottery, are ideal ways to collect without making a major investment in furnishings.

twig *branches as* drapery rods

Decorate your living room in French garden style with a mix of the rustic and refined. Here, the wrought iron daybed sets a fanciful mood that's reinforced by the skirted table and draperies. Accent with leaf-trimmed lamp shades.

Contemporary style warms up to the outdoors, too, when you start with the sleek, overscaled pieces often associated with homes and gardens in Southern California. Here, a woven storage ottoman doubles as a table for armchairs.

re-create *resort* chic

age-worn *bench* relaxes

Re-create the refined ambience of the formal garden in your foyer with a gently distressed, English-style outdoor bench. The delicate shape pairs nicely with dark woods and traditional furniture. Add a blooming plant for color.

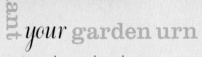

plant *your* garden urn

One great piece makes a garden-style room.
Look for a large outdoor urn, pot, or planter for
plants or seasonal flowers. An overscaled basket
for books or magazines works as an appropriate
accent for this comfortable reading nook.

decorate *two spaces* as one

Unify your porch and living room by painting
indoor and outdoor furniture in crisp, summery
white. Mismatched wood pieces, such as
this small desk and chair, enjoy renewed style
courtesy of fresh paint and perky fabric.

start with a *colorful* floral

When you enjoy bright colors, look for a floral
fabric in your favorite shades. Here, the cotton
print sets the clear red and paler green scheme
that's enhanced by the distressed wood shelves
and reclaimed desk and office chair.

paint *your* park bench

What could be a friendlier way to welcome guests to your home than a bench, painted classic green, in your entry hall? Add trimmed floral pillows and a woven, cotton rag rug for comfort and fresh, outdoor colors.

accent red *with* prints

*Lovers of deep hues choose dark walls that
create a dramatic canvas for floral prints,
painted porcelains, and majolica-style pottery
pieces. Fabrics in the pale, tea-dyed look and
quilts translate cottage charm to a city setting.*

Paint your walls in a cheerful yellow and detail below the chair rail with a French blue trellis and stylized flowers painted freehand. With this much spirit, simplify furnishings with blue and white plates for art and white wicker for seating.

add roses to *a painted* trellis

armillary *sundial* **as art**

Originally used by French astronomers, handsome iron sundials have long graced formal European and American gardens. Bring one inside as a focal point for a serene living room of soft neutrals, pottery, and seasonal flowers.

The Spirit Of British Colonial

In the hot-weather outposts of their empire, the garden-loving British relaxed their dark wood furniture with light fabrics, wicker and rattan, finds from nature, and art and treasures from native cultures. And in the steamiest climates, they lived most of the year on shady verandas furnished with comfortable chairs and handy tables for drinks and books. With this blending of indoors and out, British Colonial is a popular style re-created with classic dark woods, white cottons and linens, and artifacts from many cultures and periods.

recall a *colonial* garden look

The teak garden bench, with white cotton pillows and
cushions, emulates the old-fashioned elegance of the British
Colonial period—as do dark woods, a sisal rug, and
tropical plants. Pillows and an ottoman covered in kilim
rug fragments accent with bright colors.

The Winter Garden

Paint your rooms in soothing, neutral tones as contrast to the textures of vintage garden elements. Invest in pieces, such as the drying rack to the right of the fireplace and the detailed, cast mantel urns, that set a timeless tone. A profusion of dried flowers recalls gardens of high summer.

hen you grow weary of winter, introduce garden touches and accents for the hope of spring. Collect favorite pieces, such as large hanging planters, pottery, baskets, and vintage garden tools that you can enjoy when your garden is dormant. To keep the look relaxed and uncluttered, pare your decorating to one floral fabric and your collecting to fewer, larger pieces. Instead of a profusion of houseplants, edit your look with well-trimmed topiaries in vintage urns. Add soft throws or shawls in comforting colors for extra warmth.

One Room, Two Seasons

With the elaborately framed, focal-point mirror and richly colored rugs in temporary summer storage, this living room opens to the outdoors. A slipcover on the armchair and a change in accent pillows complete the look.

s the garden changes with the season, so, too, can interiors. In this solarium-style living room, the owners pared down and lightened up to open a rich winter room to summer. In a case of decorating subtraction, they rolled up the Oriental rugs and removed the fabric screen and mirror that warm the room in winter. For an airier summer look, a white cotton slipcover dresses the armchair, and fanciful pillows accent the cane-back settee. When the air chills, the silk screen is rehung over the French doors to replicate the opulent draperies. In a nod to the garden, oversized faux bamboo frames the mirror.

Old World Garden Touches

Influenced by the strong, clean lines of Italian gardens, this dining room imparts instant outdoor character to a new suburban house. It also aptly demonstrates how new and old can live harmoniously in a garden-inspired room. Wallpaper, in shades of lemon and sunshine, emulates subtle stripes, while painted shutters ensure privacy and sun control. Hand-painted, clip-on shades detail the chandelier. A cast-off window from a salvage yard, transformed into a handsome focal-point mirror, substitutes with style for art.

welcome *with* rustic elements

*Lighten the spirits of dark dining room furniture with
garden-inspired, distressed touches. An aged, Gothic-style
window converts into a striking mirror. The cupboard
keeps plates and serving pieces handy and displays a lamp
crafted from vines, an urn, and a miniature conservatory.*

Dining With Roses

ou create a no-fail scheme for year-round garden style when you start with a floral fabric you love. Here, for a tiny dining/sitting room combination, the rose chintz sewn as the table skirt inspired the green, ivory, and raspberry color palette. The summer shades repeat as cleverly painted backgrounds for an eclectic mix of furnishings. Walls are celery green in a combed finish; the pale painted floor features an overscaled lattice pattern. Enriching the character, old pine pieces mix with 19th-century Gothic Revival-style chairs, slipcovered in a raspberry-and-ivory plaid.

patterned *greens* and pinks

Transform traditional into garden style by painting the floor
with a trellis pattern and updating furniture with cheerful
fabrics. Plaid slipcovers instantly loosen the lines of Gothic
Revival chairs, while a skirted table introduces a pretty floral
fabric in the chosen shades of spring-fresh pink and green.

Dining In The Garden

he pleasures and ease of dining alfresco can be yours every day when you decorate in an outdoor mood. With today's interest in casual entertaining, garden style relaxes a sometimes formal room and encourages guests to linger over coffee and conversation. Employ touches such as outdoor bistro chairs or window sheers for a summery feel. If your original colors are dark, lighten the mood with white, pale green, or sunny yellow walls and a baker's rack for foliage and blooming plants. Even formal dining chairs participate in the new look when you re-cover or slipcover the seats in floral or leaf motifs.

search *for curvy* garden chairs

Once the castoffs of garage sales, worn metal garden chairs now pair with tables old and new. Search for deals at secondhand shops and mix with a painted farm table. Introduce colorful linens in happy primary colors and a flag for art.

stencil *and paint* floral details

Turn castoffs into garden style by painting and detailing mismatched furniture. Here, a checkerboard motif embellishes a small table while pink paint revives an old workbench. Stenciled flowers brighten the painted floor.

Dining
In The
Garden

Design a dining room in a snap with a baker's
rack for plants and collectibles. Mix a rugged
reproduction pine table with a garden
bench, fruit-motif pillows, and metal outdoor
chairs, and a fanciful grouping comes to life.

baker's rack for display

freshen your finds with white

For summer year-round, paint your dining
room walls and furniture in soft shades of white,
and collect white planters and containers.
Accessories, plants, plates, and art stand out
against such a clean backdrop.

*For the garden spirit, revive an old drop-leaf
table with a coat of white enamel paint and pair
with reproduction dining chairs. Hang
decoratively matted, framed botanical prints and
a drying rack to enrich your outdoor theme.*

update *white* with cool green

birdhouses *for* dining art

*Group and display the finds of your collecting
passions. Decorative hanging shelves and
a country pine table display a village of
whimsical birdhouses. Worn shutters, hinged
together, serve as a rustic corner screen.*

dining *with a garden view*

Bring a bistro table inside for the year-round ambience of dining in the garden. All you need is a small table to skirt and a pair of outdoor chairs. Mix ivy with flowers in a moss-lined hanging container, and the mood is complete.

inspired by *formal* gardens

Incorporate iron terrace chairs with tie-on
cushions when your dining goal is a dressy
version of garden style. The iron repeats for the
scrolled, marble-topped table and rods for the
sheers. Ficus trees fill Chinese fish bowls.

Terrace-Style Elegance

arden style offers tasteful, timeless elements that work equally well in the dining room or on the terrace. Here, wrought iron moves from the terrace to the dining room as a counterpoint of striking black against painted white brick. Black and white toile, the French scenic print fabric, enhances the strong graphics of the scheme. Tied-on black and white geometric floral seat cushions and plaid napkins strengthen the two-tone effect. A splash of fashionable lime green enlivens with a jolt of fresh color for the table overskirt.

update *with* lime green

Classic black and white toile, the French-style print often featuring pastoral outdoor scenes, dresses dining tables both outdoors and in. Wherever you dine, brighten the mood with an overskirt and casual checkered napkins. For equally colorful and chic overskirts, try rosy pink or sunny yellow.

*the*makeover:

Before, this living room showed
potential with green walls and a
vaulted ceiling. After decorating,
a mix of lighthearted fabrics and
garden elements turned a typical
room into a woodsy retreat.

before:

Suburban Staid To Garden Fresh

In a room with little light, how do you bring the fresh air in? Although conventional wisdom may dictate bright white walls, garden-loving homeowners preferred yellow paired with green. With this colorful start, they slipcovered their sofa and chair in a garden-motif fabric and a complementary stripe. For the new look, storage cubes serve as the coffee table, and a bench holds books and magazines. Pairs of garden-center trellises, picnic baskets, and mirrors are artful accents, as are the miniature conservatories that protect plants from the elements. A contemporary version of Victorian gazing balls, terra-cotta balls on urns, blend with the wood tones and shades of green.

the makeover:

Before, this quaint cottage lacked color and charm. After, Adirondack chairs from the owner's garden and a few quick accents from retail stores work decorating magic.

before:

The Gardener's Cottage

When a dedicated, busy gardener moves her talents indoors, count on a mix of fanciful and fun—and timesaving tips. A mail-order, hydrangea-print slipcover sparks the green, cream, and natural color scheme for the living and dining rooms. A serene shade of green revives the dull walls while the brick fireplace surround, sponge-painted in shades of medium forest green, blends into the restful palette. A pair of Adirondack chairs moves indoors from the patio. For art, a section of picket fencing from the garden, detailed with an inexpensive print and antique tools, hangs over the mantel.

the makeover:

Before, Arts and Crafts-style oak built-ins dominated the dining room. After, a leaf-print wallpaper sets a stylish tone with subtle color and pattern. Window treatments on bamboo-style rods, discount store bargains, enhance the outdoor theme.

before:

The Gardener's Cottage

Classic oak bungalow built-ins and vintage oak furniture set the mood in the dining room. With these givens and the adjacent green living room, the gardener chose a subtle, leaf-patterned wallpaper. A table runner in a complementary woven fabric and tab curtains on bamboo-motif rods complete the transformation. (The unlined sheer curtains, from a discount store, were cut and hemmed to fit.) For finishing touches, inherited floral needlework in oval frames mixes with new and old pottery pieces. Shades of soft green and cream allow flowers and herbs from the garden to be the decorative focus.

The Kitchen Garden

As kitchens become true living rooms, it's only natural that they reflect how families live and entertain. And when your passion is gardening, your kitchen should reflect your interests. For a quick start, add a shelf or two at your sink window for potted herbs. Or simply use the sill for small bottles or vases filled with seasonal flowers. For more growing space, install a greenhouse window. Little accents make a difference, too. Display garden accessories and finds, such as birdhouses, watering cans, woven or wire baskets, or terra-cotta pots, on the tops of cabinets. Hang a botanical print or two to finish.

decorate *with* rustic elements

Make space for one signature garden element in your
kitchen. An oversized willow chair with colorful cushions
works here with a pine server, baskets, white pottery, and
planted terra-cotta pots as supporting players. Choose
colors, such as this sunny yellow, inspired by the outdoors.

Fresh-Air Kitchen Accents

When you introduce the garden into your kitchen, start with a terrace-style breakfast area. Even when space is tight, you'll have room for a small bistro or patio table for two. Pair with folding metal or wood chairs. Or, for the unexpected twists that make decorating a pleasure, substitute painted ladderback chairs. Add padded seat covers or cushions to set your color scheme. (Use tea towels as fabric alternatives.) If you love florals, mix or match patterns for cushions, window treatments, table linens, and decorative tea towels.

blue and white *garden* kitchen

Put a garden spin on the always
classic blue and white kitchen
with beaded-board cabinet doors
that emulate porch ceilings.
Lattice-style patterns detail
glass-front doors. An iron
chandelier with a clay pot
contributes to the ambience.

choose *country* french

When you invest in a pair of country French-style armchairs, you have the stars of a garden look. Paint a vintage, country-style bench for extra seating and decorate with touches such as classic hay rakes and wire animal baskets.

character *of worn finishes*

Turn your back door or kitchen entry into a
potting area with a dry sink or other storage
piece. Look for sturdy pieces in distressed
finishes for hints of the garden. Hang pegboards
or shelves to organize baskets and hand tools.

Sun-Filled Rooms

When you crave light, think sunroom for your family or living room. With walls of windows, your sitting and gathering space will be cheerful throughout the year. Such rooms work best with southern or eastern exposures to avoid the intense late afternoon, western sun. With technological advances, window glass or professionally applied film blocks damaging rays to reduce sun exposure. Window treatments, from shutters to blinds or shades lined with sun-resistant fabrics, stylishly solve the problem of too much sun.

the softly *furnished* sunroom

When you spend a lot of time in your sunroom, treat it as
your living room with comfortable upholstered pieces,
botanical-motif pillows, lamps and draperies, and your
favorite collectibles and vases. Dried topiaries, in decorative
urns or clay pots, impart sophisticated, yet no-care touches.

Sunny Spaces

un porches, sunspaces, sunrooms, conservatories. Whatever they are called, these glassed-in rooms give you summer all year long—at least in one room. It's no wonder that the sun-starved English popularized the idea of conservatories. Their Victorian-era sunspaces turned working greenhouses into architecturally interesting rooms. On a more modest scale, glassed-in porches transform fresh-air summer rooms into year-round sitting and reading areas. With a mix of furniture and lighting, such rooms are often family favorites.

mix fabrics *for easy* decorating

Energize a white sun porch with key touches
of the bright and bold. Cushions in tailored
stripes, country French-style cotton pillows,
and a perky lampshade spark the scheme.
Hang roll-up bamboo shades for sun control.

folk art *adds* character

Look for special pieces of folk art, such as this
miniature church, and an unusual small table or
two when you decorate a sunroom. A painted
floor and pots of grass and flowers keep summer
spirits alive on the coldest of days.

scale up *for* ornaments **with impact**

*When your sunroom is spacious, make it a true
garden room with ornaments from the outdoors.
Shop for handsome artifacts, such as armillary
sundials and worn urns on stands, to group with
reproductions or new art and ornaments.*

sporty stripes with *pretty* florals

*Bring your woven rattan chaise inside and
team florals with colorful awning stripes. A
floor lamp and small, painted side table for tea
complete the reading nook. Decorate simply
with plants and your favorite gardening books.*

garden *bench* as coffee table

*Simple touches warm a sunroom. Relax a
tailored white sofa with an aged garden bench
for drinks and collectibles. For art in a window-
filled room, elevate a folk art birdhouse or a
garden ornament on a porch balustrade.*

The Conservatory Sun Porch

Painted and planted, a metal mini greenhouse brings a kaleidoscope of colors into this nature-inspired sun porch. Furnishings enhance the outdoor spirit with salvaged logs recycled into a pair of tables. For planter-style tables, the tops of both logs are hollowed out. One, planted with petunias and ivy, is an accent table while the other, lined with moss, serves as the coffee table. Branches double as rods for curtains, held in place with stones on the window ledge. Antique wicker, upholstered in florals, completes the setting.

recycle *forest* finds

In this conservatory-style sun porch, a mini greenhouse
planted with spring flowers works as the decorative accent
for a setting created from tables and curtain rods rescued
from a storm-damaged tree. Dark wicker, dressed with a
green and white floral fabric, blends with this woodsy setting.

A Collector's Retreat

If you love to collect and to garden, transform your passions into your own personal and pretty style. In this bedroom and adjacent sunroom, one wonderful piece—a green iron bed with tiny painted flowers—sets the mood of a spring garden. A rose-covered, circa 1940s bedspread and fragments of antique tablecloths and old fabrics made into pillows dress the bed. The worn fragment, valued for its patina of age as well as for its shape, works as the valance. An antique garden trellis adds architectural interest, as does the old shutter on the opposite side of the antique Victorian wire plant stand.

When you collect, focus your finds on your favorite colors and fabrics. Botanical art as well as tole-painted trays and vases are easy-to-find collectibles that mix well with wire stands and architectural fragments. Group like-colored vases or other similar pieces together for the most impact.

live with *your* passions

terms of *floral* endearment

Group your garden collectibles for the prettiest display. Floral hatboxes, vintage suitcases stacked as a table, and decorative, hanging corner shelves create storage and organization. A salvaged trellis displays art while the wire plant stand holds plants and magazine-filled metal buckets.

For The Love Of The Lily

When you love a flower, enjoy your favorite all year long in your own bedroom. Here, the pretty English-style lily chintz, repeated for the window treatments and duvet, inspired the lovely large scale "corner charm" lily motif. (The corner charm translates, in floral language, into a grouping of flowers at a corner.) The lilies painted in the four corners of the room accentuate the wide band of cream paint above the parchment-colored walls. A framed lithograph poster above the bed reinforces the soft, sophisticated scheme.

garden *of calm* sophistication

When your goal is a bedroom for soothing repose, introduce an armchair or chaise for reading and pale floral fabrics as accents to neutral wall colors. Rather than fill your room with collections, choose only several large pieces, such as this finely detailed garden urn containing a chic white orchid.

Sleeping With Salvage

his serene bedroom, decorated with architectural salvage, translates fragments into an indoor-outdoor scheme. The bed, constructed from two old columns, features a roof gable hung picture-frame style from the wall. The dressing table, a flea market find, is covered with a vintage pillowcase, while a porch balustrade finds new life as a lamp. As the translucent shade, cheese-cloth covers the wire frame made from a discarded lampshade. For elements as art, old cast iron heater grates dangle stylishly above the cloth-covered table.

fragments of *long-ago* times

When you love vintage architectural fragments,
go beyond the decorative to furniture crafted
from your finds. The trunk, from pressed ceiling
tin, pairs with a bed made from salvage and a
table base made from an aged column capital.

Bed &
Bath
Bowers

Create a garden of serenity with a bedroom that speaks of the spring garden. Surround yourself with the flowers or garden motifs you love. Look for fabric, wallpaper, prints, or art with your favorite motifs. Garden style is equally engaging in a child's bedroom or guest retreat. Be playful in your little one's room with a mural in a favorite theme. For guests, create calm with easy touches such as a wicker chaise and a basket filled with gardening magazines.

wallpaper a *flower* garden

For a quick transformation
to garden style, choose an old-
fashioned, floral wallpaper
for a bedroom. A cornice with
softly draping fabric, hung
above the bed, enhances
the romantic, under-the-eaves
appeal of this cozy room.

the painterly *cottage* bedroom

Pale blue and white wicker set the cool scheme for a bedroom with flower-garden details. The cabinet doors of the chimney breast and the floor are stenciled with stylized flowers. The ceramic elephant garden stool doubles as a table.

Bed &
Bath
Bowers

Dress a four-poster bed in a pretty mix of
floral linens and ruffled pillows. Add botanical
art, a decorative lampshade for an urn
lamp, flowers in a decorated pottery vase—
and garden style enlivens a traditional setting.

colonial *style* florals

ribbon and *rose* motifs

Convert a vintage chest for bath storage.
Brighten with fresh white enamel, and hand-
paint a spring bouquet, gathered by a painted
ribbon. Hang a decoratively framed mirror
above to enhance the always-spring theme.

unify *with paper* and fabric

Decorate an under-the-eaves bedroom the
easiest way possible with a floral wallpaper
recalling a bygone era and matching fabric for
the balloon shade. Finish with an oval mirror
and pottery vase filled with fresh flowers.

charm *of tiny* garden touches

Enjoy quaint miniatures such as these
child-size and doll-size chairs. Plant a rustic
container with grass seeds for a touch of
spring. The folk art, flower garden quilt is a
pleasing complement to these cottage touches.

sleeping *in the* garden

Simple pieces in stained and painted wood infuse a country-style bedroom with the casual charm of the summer garden. The bed is dressed in a cheerful mix of new and vintage linens while framed art leans casually against the wall.

outdoor *sconces* for soft light

For a bedroom as a hidden garden, choose a
shade of mellow plaster for the painted walls.
Leave the windows bare or use shutters for
privacy. An armoire in an aged finish
contributes to the Old World garden look.

A Touch Of Victorian Style

When spaces are cramped, think storage with style. In this dressing room, straw hats are hung for easy access and decoration. And the floral skirt provides concealed storage. The bedroom, too, decoratively makes the most of a tight space with a collection of tole-painted trays as botanical-style art. The trellis-patterned carpet, delicately painted bed, bamboo side table, and tufted uphol-stered chair recall subtle touches of Victorian garden style. Cafe curtains, topped with a valance, contribute another floral to the feminine scheme.

garden *hats* and tole trays

Prized by garden-style decorators, tole trays balance palettes
with sophisticated touches of black. Look for
vintage trays in an array of sizes and shapes at antique and
secondhand stores and some garden design shops.
Reproductions are sold by some gift shops and catalogs.

Down By The River

Keep it simple and easy to manage when you plan a room for a preschool or elementary student. As children's rooms tend to be small and the clutter of toys and books large, use the walls and furniture as canvases to paint pretty outdoor or garden scenes—and limit accessories and art. Decorative painters, art instructors, or art students are ready sources of talent to translate outdoor ideas into playful rooms, such as these scenes inspired by classic children's stories. Or you may prefer to stencil or wallpaper a border in a garden motif.

Turn to classic children's literature for themes that bring
nature and the garden inside. Use soft colors, such
as these shades of pink and green, for a pretty girl's room.
Fill pots with blooming plants or easy-grow houseplants
for the young gardener to tend in a sunny window.

draw in a *soothing* outdoor scene

Baby's Garden Of Verses

hat could be happier to nurture your little one than a nursery in a garden? This baby's room features the cheerful mix of painted motifs by a decorative artist, clever fabric treatments, and playful touches. Three of the walls are color washed to a mottled sky blue; the fourth is a sunny yellow. The artist drew freehand, then painted the partridge in a pear tree, topiaries in urns, sunburst pediment, lattice, and picket fence. Valances, designed with the casual appeal of outdoor awnings, and fabric shades add to the charm. The topiary fabric repeats for an accent pillow that softens the painted porch rocker.

sew and paint *a garden* nursery

With a theme of topiaries and the partridge in a pear
tree, this fun-filled nursery ensures its young resident
will wake up in a perpetually cheerful setting. The antique
iron bed, dressed in an array of bright fabrics, meets
safety standards—slats are less than 2⅜ inches apart.

LIVING

The GARDEN *Life*

For the gardener or the lover of garden style, indoors and out blend seamlessly as one space to nurture and decorate. Boundaries disappear as these five evocative homes and gardens speak of their owners' love for nature— and of the art and craft of gardening and decorating.

As gardeners delight in sharing their plants and knowledge, so, too, do garden-style decorators share their homes. On the West Coast, Gail Miller's cottage in Carmel, California, brims with the fresh-air spirit of natural woods and white fabrics. French doors open the serene interiors to the dining terrace.

Across the continent, a new garden ages with style as the striking grounds for a restored 1820s Connecticut house and shop. Based on owner Michael Trapp's travels, the plan mixes garden history and his favorite elements.

In Texas, gardener/decorator Charlotte Comer ignores distinctions between inside and outside as she turns her family's bungalow into a cool haven from the long Dallas summers. Her two outdoor living rooms ensure shady spots for sitting morning and afternoon.

Ryan Gainey, a garden designer, author, and shop owner, works with his own Atlanta, Georgia, home, garden, and shop as canvases for his creativity. A pioneer in popularizing garden-style decorating, Gainey evolves his style to create environments attuned to nature and the rhythms of the seasons.

In West Des Moines, Iowa, writer/editor Elvin McDonald's four-season, formal garden transforms the character of a suburban lot with seasonally planted beds and garden structures. In the process, McDonald opens his garden to good causes—and inspires a neighborhood to share outdoor spaces.

COUNTRY
In The
SUBURBS

Elvin McDonald

An opera singer by education, Elvin McDonald creates his expressive English-European-style garden compositions from his lifelong love of music.

"Music is the basis of my gardening," says the editor, author, and garden designer. "As repetition is part of the composition of music, I repeat colors, shapes, and textures when I compose a garden. Like music, a well-thought-out garden design has a climax, a crescendo." Today, McDonald—a gardener since his Oklahoma childhood—plants and prunes on a suburban corner lot in West Des Moines, Iowa. But for 30 years, he gardened in a New York City high-rise. "I painted the walls of my apartment the color of wet, unglazed terra-cotta pots and made a bamboo plant arbor so I could have coffee in the garden. Visitors would always remark how they felt they were in a garden with all my plants."

In a year of intensive effort, the senior staff editor at *Traditional Home* magazine has designed and supervised installation of a remarkably detailed landscape—and decorated his home. His landscape plan transforms a typical backyard into a four-season garden with a dining pavilion (*opposite*) and a garden house. Rather than close off the garden, McDonald worked with fellow gardener David Kvitne to design a round moongate that allows sidewalk joggers and walkers views of the ever-changing landscape. "When you invite people in, they are respectful," McDonald says. "I enjoy that people are interested, that they want to know about the garden."

As the garden changes with the seasons, so do the interiors. Plants and furniture, including the tables made from tree limbs and bamboo canes, move inside and out—from house to deck to garden and back again. In cool months, plants from the deck crowd the sunny windows and find winter quarters on wooden stools. In spring, forced bulbs and branches from flowering trees bloom with the hope of the growing season. By summer, roses from the garden create a kitchen still life of bottles and blooms. "I love the change of seasons," McDonald says. "It forces you to change, and change is stimulating. When I moved here, I decided to start a new life. I have, with my home and garden."

"Like music, a *well-thought-out* garden

McDonald "ages" his suburban deck with
salvaged architectural fragments for trim, while
he creates pleasant spots for seating with
benches in shady nooks. June lilies enhance the
garden, planned for blooms through the growing
season. Pots of annuals add strategic color from
spring until they move inside at frost.

design has a *climax*, a crescendo."

A circular moongate in the privacy fence
welcomes walkers and joggers to share ever-
changing views of the garden. McDonald scours
flea markets and shops for his collections of folk
art birdhouses and vintage watering cans. Birds,
too, love the garden and are guests at the rustic
feeder, which is easily visible from the house.

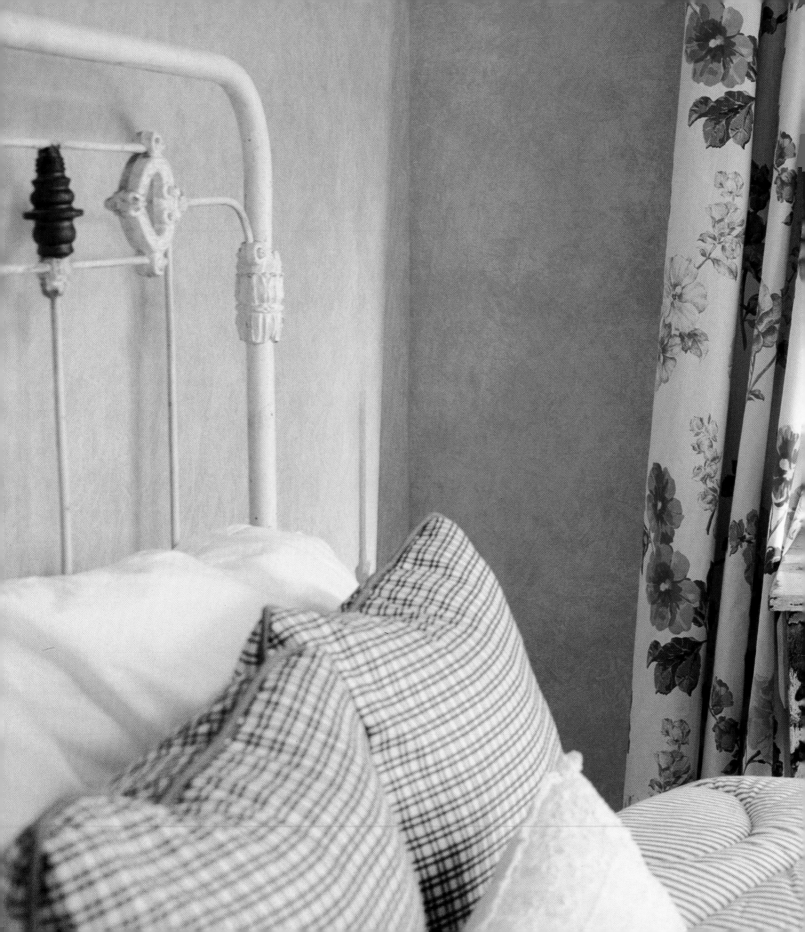

McDonald infused his guest room with the warmth of his summer garden. A pretty floral print, hung decoratively, sets the color palette with delicately sponged walls and a gently distressed table accented by white and silver.

Everyday objects evolve into things of style and
beauty under McDonald's deft touch. Bottles
large and small reflect light below a sunny
window, while a pair of bottles under an aged
table double as vases for dried allium from the
garden. Worn shutters detail a bookcase,
stocked with gardening and garden design books.

Favorite plants mix with decorative finials and pottery on the round, skirted dining table. Long-lasting orchids in decorative, antique-finish pots enliven the carefully arranged display of fruit and foliage when McDonald entertains.

they felt they were *in a garden* with all my plants."

Brimming with plants, the low living room windowsill doubles as a conservatory. A striking metal ornament from the garden finds new life as indoor art. Roses from McDonald's own garden fill an array of everyday bottles, stylishly arranged in the kitchen window.

BUNGALOW
On A
BUDGET

Charlotte Comer

"I don't think of inside and outside as separate," says Charlotte Comer of her Dallas, Texas, bungalow and garden. "Instead, I try to create a total environment for what interests me." A collector, traveler, and gardener, the interior designer decorates her 1935 vintage home with her interests and passions. She started with the deck she and her husband, Edward, use as an outdoor living room from February to November. "When we can, we live outside," she says. "Our garden means quiet and serenity—and it adds two rooms to our house. We planned it so we would have shady areas morning or afternoon."

After trips to France, Comer's con-cepts of gardening and decorating have evolved. "I've been greatly influenced by the way the French do their gardens. I used to plant a lot more flowers. Now I'm interested in more architecturally shaped green shrubs, which the French use, that look good in summer and winter. In the summer, I plant flowers in the pots I collect when I travel. I look for pots with raised designs or patterns, which make them more interesting."

France also has influenced her appreciation of the effects of light. "I noticed the quality of light in France, which is very striking and luminous," she says. "I began to appreciate how light translates into paintings. When I do interiors, I bring the light of the garden inside."

For her own bungalow, the light-filled rooms are neutral backdrops for archi-tectural fragments, art, and textiles. "I've used garden elements as structure, to set the stage for the things I love," she explains. "Using architectural elements inside seems to me to be an obvious way to blend the house and garden. I collect from all over the world. I search for old textiles, art, and things with history."

In the living room, a window grate with distressed shutters from Morocco substitutes for more conventional art over the mantel, while old porch columns with layers of peeling paint add other points of interest as pedestals. The white dining room, equally eclectic, includes white creamware and porce-lains. Turn-of-the-century pressed weeds and flowers, collected on trips to France, are reminders of the long-standing tradition of decorating with nature.

"When I do *interiors,* I try to bring the

Comer created an instant console table for her deck from two cast, classical-style bases and beveled ½-inch-thick, tempered glass. For variations in height, she elevates pots on decorative feet, available at nurseries, garden centers, and garden design shops.

light of the *French* garden inside."

The low-key, relaxed family room features subtle garden-motif touches, such as the botanical prints and pottery in the corner cupboard. Antique bamboo chairs with deep cushions recall old-fashioned sun porches.

Comer chose spider-back dining chairs and
a lacy, open-weave tablecloth to keep the look
open and easy in her white dining room.
Vases and carafes filled with her garden
flowers make an easy, elegant centerpiece.

The idea of the all-white garden translates into Comer's
stylishly eclectic dining room, decorated with creamware,
pottery, and porcelains. Because they are all white,
the disparate objects and shapes work together without
distracting color. Dried ferns stand out in this setting.

A soft white background acts as the canvas for collected architectural salvage and vintage furnishings. A fragment from afar, a window grate with shutters from Morocco leans against the chimney breast. Porch columns as plant pedestals and artfully arranged, vintage chairs contribute to the indoor-outdoor spirit.

"I've used

garden *elements* as the structure to set the stage *for the things I love.*"

A floral fabric detailed with butterflies inspires the color
scheme for Comer's tiny guest room, decorated
with linens, fabrics with urn motifs, and plates. The lined
bed canopy and unlined sheer hangings attach to
the metal frame with drapery rings to create a cozy nook.

NATURE
In The
CITY

Ryan Gainey

Styles in art and landscaping come and go, but for 25 years Ryan Gainey, garden designer, shop owner, and author, has based his life and his work on the home and garden as one harmonious, integrated space. For the past 16 of those years, Gainey has lived and gardened in Decatur, a close-in suburb of Atlanta.

A horticulturist by education and a lifelong student of the international history of gardening, Gainey says his ideas on gardening and on indoor and outdoor spaces have been "emancipated" over time. "When I talk about emancipation, I'm talking about freeing myself of distinctions of what should be outside and what should be inside. My clients share my philosophy that the garden is integral to the house and vice versa. In my mind, it's impossible to separate your environments. Unifying the indoors with the garden and responding to nature is how I live and work, how I begin my garden designs for clients."

For his own bungalow, the garden designer surrounds the house with gardens that screen for privacy and create a series of outdoor rooms. Structural materials, such as fencing and arbors crafted from logs and branches, and stacked stone walls and columns, meld the constructed into the landscape.

Indicative of how Gainey lives, the gardens are visible through the porch from his dining room and kitchen. With the stone terrace as the transition, the garden and bungalow are one space for living and entertaining. No other houses are seen, enhancing the feeling of a hidden mountain retreat.

As his gardens have evolved over time, so, too, has the bungalow. Colors reflect the textures, materials, and shades of nature—from the deciduous magnolia leaves peeling from the ceiling in the sitting room above the painted floor, to the Native American baskets and pressed-fern, linen screen. "Elegance is making the choice of restraint," adds Gainey. "I choose very carefully the objects I live with. My work and my environment bring me as close as possible to nature. I remember one of my professors used to remind us that when you walk through the garden, the garden should walk with you. That's what I work toward wherever I am."

"My clients share my *philosophy* that the garden

is integral to *the house* and vice versa."

Gainey has spent 16 years designing and cultivating the lush
gardens that shelter his Atlanta house. An authority on
regional plants, Gainey chooses varieties for blooms through
the long, hot Southern growing season. The fountain, crafted
from a hand pump, recalls his rural Southern heritage.

"My work and *my environment* bring

me as close as

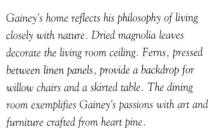

Gainey's home reflects his philosophy of living closely with nature. Dried magnolia leaves decorate the living room ceiling. Ferns, pressed between linen panels, provide a backdrop for willow chairs and a skirted table. The dining room exemplifies Gainey's passions with art and furniture crafted from heart pine.

ossible to nature."

CASUAL *In* CALIFORNIA

The temperate climate of the Carmel Valley on the Monterey Peninsula encourages homes open to the views and breezes. Such a setting for home and garden is a natural for Gail and Raymie Miller, who lived in Hawaii for 14 years before moving back to the mainland.

"We wanted to re-create the same indoor-outdoor feeling we had on the islands," Miller says. "We're happiest in sunshine; this climate attracts people who like the outdoors." This combination of climate and setting lured the Millers to a run-down hunting retreat, which they restored as their year-round, easy-living, indoor-outdoor home.

Gail Miller

With views of rolling hills and large oak trees and mature plants on the property, the Millers worked with a remodeling plan that opened the cottage to the natural landscape. French doors, added during the remodeling, lead from the dining room to the lanai, a Hawaiian term for an open-air living area. For entertaining, the dining room and lanai work as one space, with massive wood dining tables both indoors and out. As openness is always a priority, Gail Miller had a long, narrow Douglas fir dining table constructed from salvaged barn wood. "We liked it because the light wood doesn't distract from the view," she says. The only ornamentation in the dining area is a stone urn.

Throughout the interior, the natural wood and white palette, with minimal accessories, reflects the casual lifestyle of the sunny area. Instead of pattern and color, textures and scale create interest and comfort. In keeping with the subtle design and minimalist approach, a few key accessories allude to the outdoors. Topiary forms, displayed on the living room console, were custom-made with a rusted finish. Oversize hurricane lamps found in a nearby Carmel shop are light yet large-scale and dramatic accents. Orchids, the only indoor plants, remind the Millers of island living.

In the same mood, French doors open the master bedroom to the outside. The Millers left doors bare and arranged the bed so they wake up to a view of their pool and the mountains. The only draperies, which can be closed for privacy, are around the four-poster bed.

Woven dining chairs introduce texture into the calm white
and natural wood indoor-outdoor decorating scheme. With a
view blessed by mountains and trees, windows remain
uncovered. Decorative elements, chosen for large scale and
shape, balance the openness without distracting clutter.

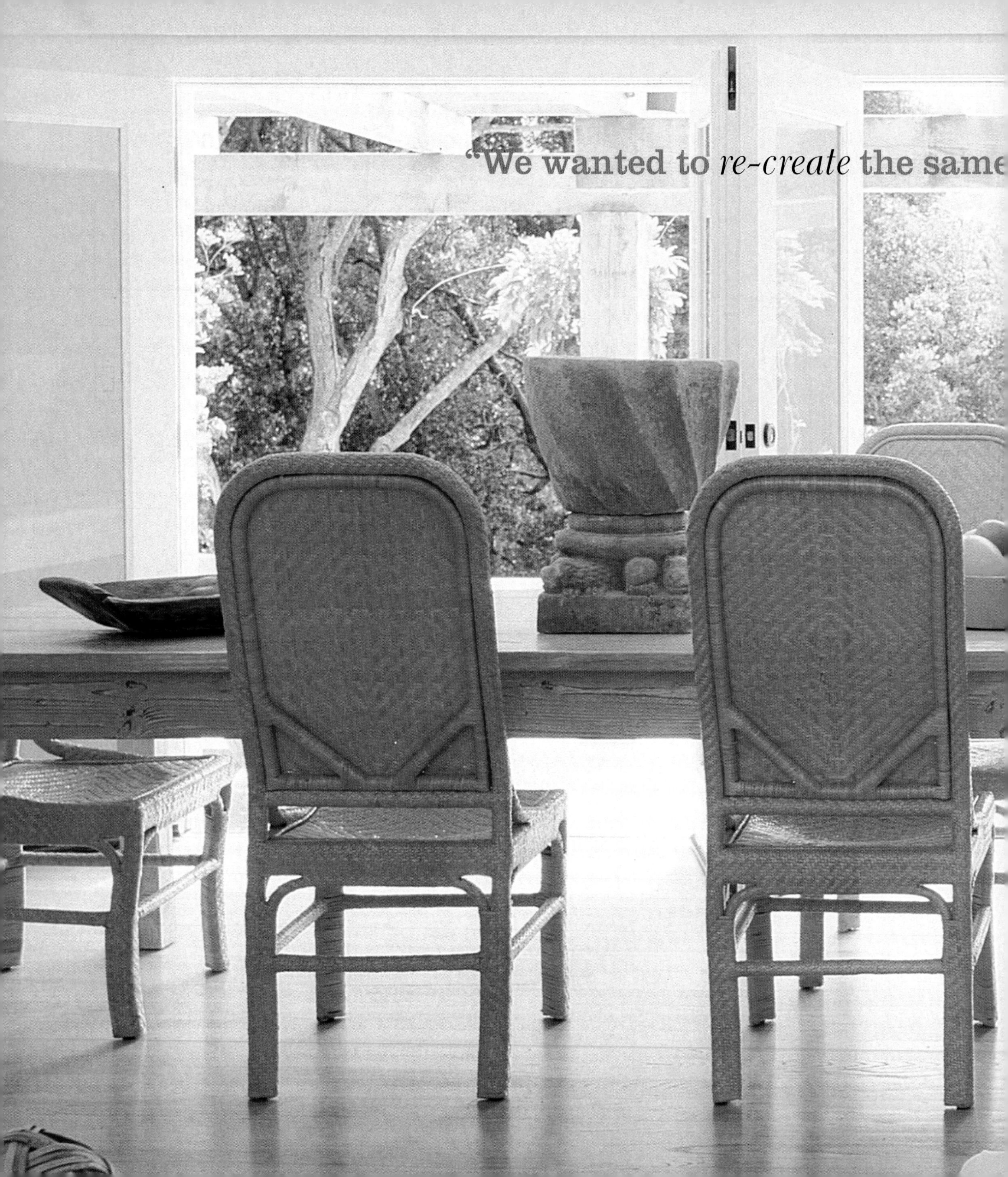

"We wanted to *re-create* the same

indoor-outdoor
feeling we had *on the islands*."

Large-scale furnishings and accessories and
neutral upholstered pieces are hallmarks of
California decorating. With so much plant life
outside, the cast decorative urn and the glazed
olive oil jar on the floor are left empty.

"We're happiest *in sunshine;* this

The living room, in a white and natural palette, reflects the overscaled, uncluttered look of California homes and landscapes. Arranged with a leaning mirror and pottery plate, a topiary form lends a sculptural element. In such a temperate climate, Gail Miller concentrates her gardening on outdoor plants.

climate attracts

people *who like* the outdoors."

The Millers wake every morning to sounds of the birds
and views of the garden. Gail Miller designed the
bed hangings so the airy, tie-on draperies can be closed for
privacy. The pared-down furnishings from natural woods
reflect the influence of Eastern philosophies on California.

OLD WORLD *In* CONNECTICUT

For eight years, Michael Trapp has artfully aged his West Cornwall, Connecticut, home and garden. And with every urn from Crete or recycled timber or stone, the house and garden retreat further back into time.

"I wanted to make the house and garden seem as though they were 500 years old," says the garden and furniture designer and antique store owner. "I'm good at making things look old." Part of this comes from Trapp's background as a landscape architecture student and junk shop owner and part from his love of classic gardens. "I've traveled quite a bit in Europe, and I love different parts of different cultures. I like the

Michael Trapp

plant material in English gardens, the feeling of French gardens, the lines of Italian gardens. You can't go in and clip out part of a vista in Rome or dig up the little bridge in Giverny and bring it home. But you can reflect the sensibility of the passion and experience in what you do in your own home and garden."

Whether he is working on his own evolving garden, surrounding an 1820 clapboard house and later carriage house, or designing for friends or clients, Trapp approaches gardening and garden design as creative self-expression. "I don't think there are any rules to follow," he says. "While I have things I'm passionate about, there aren't right and wrong ways to garden and decorate. It's better and more fun to experiment more and be creative. If you don't like some-

thing, change it. No one is going to arrest you if you make an error in taste."

This experimentation in his home leads to paths to explore, tall plantings such as the late-summer hollyhocks, and views inside and out that change with the seasons and times of day. "I love natural things and art," Trapp says. "The combination is what my gardens and interiors are about. I don't distinguish between the outside and the inside, between what materials or architectural fragments I use where. In the summer, I leave all the doors open, and the leaves blow across the stone floor. I design furniture from old architectural elements and give them new life. I change something, and the light changes. Every day my home and my garden are different, which is wonderful."

"I wanted to make *the house* and garden seem as

though *they were* 500 years old"

Trapp designs with stone, architectural fragments, and vintage garden furniture. Not bound by rules, Trapp introduces overscaled natural elements, such as the giant clamshell, seashells, and antlers, as counterpoints to the crystal chandelier in his own conservatory-style dining room.

"I leave *all the* doors open, and the leaves *blow across* the stone floor."

Elements of the European garden decorate the
breakfast room. Notable pieces include the
miniature conservatory on the worn, turned-leg
table and the etched-glass bell jar on the dining
table. Dried flowers are from Trapp's garden.

"I design *furniture from* old architectural

Trapp re-created the faded elegance of an Old World villa for his master bedroom and bath. Columns, column capitals, and urns contribute to the blending of periods and styles. Spanish moss sways above the metal tub, while shells are arranged in an elevated metal urn. The shower curtain attaches behind crown molding.

elements and *give them new life.*"

IDEAS, SOURCES,

Inspirations

cro
nin

hen you are ready to decorate, visit garden design shops, which offer ideas, antiques, art, and ornaments to create your own indoor-outdoor look. As most shops are locally owned and managed, expect the looks and merchandise to be as different and diverse as their towns

and owners. Just as there are no rights and wrongs in garden-style decorating, there's no standard merchandise in garden design shops—which makes them all the more enjoyable and interesting to browse.

Some shops offer cut flowers, perennials, houseplants, seasonal annuals, and practical garden tools as part of their merchandise mix. Others specialize in outdoor-indoor decorative items, such as birdbaths, urns, pots, and planters. Often, shops carry a mix of reproduction and vintage items, with imports of both the new and old. You'll also find shops that carry garden art and ornaments crafted by local or regional artists—and shops that sell pottery, linens, candles, and accessories for outdoor dining and entertaining.

Many of the larger shops feature an array of outdoor furniture, such patio tables and chairs and benches that work equally well inside. You may find stores that sell only new or reproduction furniture, or shops that mix the new with the fashionably aged. Salvage companies, secondhand and antique stores, flea markets, and even garage sales and tag sales are worthwhile sources of architectural fragments, garden ornaments, and outdoor furniture. And don't forget antique shows, including those known for vintage garden ornaments. Keep your eyes open as you shop and travel. You never know when you'll spot furnishings and elements of garden style.

The East Coast

arden design sources are as varied as the East Coast landscape. New York City offers choices from shops featuring European antiques to funky venues for planters, aged furniture, and salvaged tools. Day trips from the city to Hudson, New York, or to West Cornwall and Woodbury, Connecticut, yield shops with fine antiques and bargain finds. From Maine to Washington, D.C., you'll find shops packed with ideas and treasures. Some resort areas are seasonal, so call to be sure your destination is open. (See pages 210–219 for listings.)

elegant imports in New York

Internationally known Treillage attracts garden design lovers who have an eye for European ornaments and pottery, iron outdoor furniture, antiques, and fine architectural fragments. In warm weather, the landmark's courtyard expands shopping possibilities—and offers a wealth of design ideas.

blooms *in* the capital city

*Marston Luce, Washington, D.C., combines
the new and the old with comfortable furniture
and blooming plants for displays geared to
interior spaces as well as suburban gardens and
city courtyards and terraces.*

source

for garden antiques

Located in New York's Soho neighborhood,
Gray Gardens Antiques sells vintage elements,
ornaments, outdoor furniture, and accessories.
Garden-style lovers frequent the shop for
inspiration on displays with unusual finds.

Well-known among Washington, D.C., garden design shops, Marston Luce combines topiaries and blooming plants with high-style furniture, architectural fragments, and garden ornaments.

style *with* topiaries

antique *outdoor* elements

Well-arranged antique garden furniture and chic accessories are signatures of Treillage, on the Upper East Side, one of a number of well-known garden design shops in New York. See pages 216–217 for shops throughout the city.

garden *treasure* hunt

Michael Trapp, a West Cornwall, Connecticut, antique dealer and garden designer, selects urns, ornaments, and furniture for his namesake shop. An authentic patina of age is the hallmark of the garden elements he chooses.

The South

urtured by a climate conducive to outdoor living, garden style is a tradition for both everyday Southern living and special-occasion entertaining. Older cities, such as Charleston and New Orleans, are justly famous for their gardens and private courtyards. With these legacies, garden design shops throughout the South offer ornaments and elements. Antique shops and architectural salvage houses are other sources of garden furnishings, while a growing number of shops feature work by regional artists. (See pages 210–219.)

focal points *for the* landscape

The Elegant Earth in Mountain Brook, a
suburb of Birmingham, Alabama, imports aged
European pots, urns, and decorative accessories
and also sells fine American garden antiques and
ornaments from its shop and courtyard.

Long associated with garden-style decorating, Ryan Gainey & Co. in Atlanta is a resource for the work of regional artists and artisans as well as imported garden furnishings and one-of-a-kind outdoor ornaments.

custom designs *for the* table

elements *for* indoor dining

Hollyhock, Atlanta, Georgia, features fun and funky elements and furnishings, including linens, pottery, and tabletop accessories. Innovative displays and creative combinations are part of the appeal.

Wickets, in scenic Middleburg, Virginia, sells a wide variety of old-fashioned indoor and outdoor furniture as well as tools and ornaments. The shop's clever displays are well worth the short drive from Washington, D.C.

easy *country* gardening

accents as *design* details

Clever and practical accessories, such as these drawer pulls, are for sale at Christopher Glenn in Homewood, a suburb of Birmingham, Alabama. Decorative cast planters and plaques add to the fanciful mix of the old and new.

French **and** English

Tourists and locals alike frequent Charleston Gardens in the beautiful old South Carolina coastal city. The shop and mail-order catalog specialize in imports from well-known French and English garden design sources.

vintage *in* Virginia

The always-changing merchandise at Wickets, in Middleburg, Virginia, offers a mix of well-worn furniture and accessories for home and garden. Metal chairs, rustic tables, old tools, and topiaries are included.

fragments *and* finds

Twig House, in East Vienna, Virginia, replicates the funky chic of flea market shopping with architectural salvage, vintage furniture, and garden-motif pottery. Changing merchandise displays, flowers, and old toys contribute to the atmosphere of casual shopping amid the stacked treasures.

The Midwest

From the neighborhoods of Minneapolis-St. Paul and Chicago to small towns and resort villages, garden design shops are destinations across the Midwest. Their products reflect the variety of the region's homes and lifestyles. Shops in large cities sell planters and furniture for lofts and apartment terraces, while small-town and country stores offer bargains in old tools and outdoor furniture. Chicago and Kansas City, with architectural salvage firms, are meccas for shoppers attracted to fragments and aged garden furniture.

furnishings for *garden* room

Casabella, in Edina, a suburb of Minneapolis, Minnesota, stocks furnishings and accents from elegant European imports and garden-motif pillows to fashionable wire accessories, baskets, and unusual architectural fragments.

Metal tables, accessories for outdoor
entertaining, fresh flowers, and even candle
chandeliers are all part of the mix at Trapp and
Company in Kansas City, Missouri. Terra-
cotta ornaments contribute to the presentation.

flowers *and* finds

quaint *cottage* style

Visitors enjoy the seasonal mix of ideas and
merchandise, including dried and fresh flowers
and topiary forms, at Camrose Hill Flower
Studio and Farm Shop, in Stillwater, Minnesota,
a scenic small town near Minneapolis.

With stores nationwide, including two
Chicago-area locations, Smith & Hawken is
known for finely crafted tools, planters,
furniture, and ornaments. See page 213
for additional catalog information.

mail-order *sources* **for garden style**

visit *shops* **for ideas**

Known for striking displays and clever design
presentations, Jayson's Home & Garden
in Chicago is a resource for reproduction urns,
ornaments, accessories, vintage tools, and a
wide choice of plants and containers.

art for *garden* rooms

The array of merchandise in room settings gives
Camrose Hill, in Stillwater, Minnesota, the feel
of a charming Victorian-era cottage. Vintage
scrolled iron chairs and terrace tables are always
in demand for indoor settings and for terraces.

A New Leaf Studio & Garden, in Chicago,
stocks a wide variety of garden-style accessories,
such as colorful glass vases in an array of sizes,
and artfully dried topiaries from seasonal flowers.

hot colors *and* chic shapes

for ornaments

Salvage One Architectural Artifacts, in Chicago, carries fragments of all descriptions as well as vintage garden furniture and ornaments. The salvage company is a regional source for large urns, wrought iron fencing, and finials.

The
West &
Southwest

arden design shops reflect the vast differences in climate, lifestyle, history—and gardening—of the West and Southwest from the Pacific Coast to Arizona, Texas, and Oklahoma. In California, shops offer choices from Napa Valley stores with Italian and French influences to the Mexican garden art and pottery of San Diego. In the Southwest, the cities and small towns of Texas are equally diverse with shops selling garden-style finds from fine European imports to Mexican iron work and gently aged country pieces.

outdoor *entertaining* ideas

*Vanderbilt and Company is a Napa Valley,
California, source for European
accessories, pottery, and dinnerware as well
as painted and iron furniture. The open-air
shopping reflects the mild, sunny climate.*

old *world* ambience

Decorated in European villa style,
Kay O'Toole Antiques and Eccentricities, in
Houston, Texas, is known as an elegant venue
for iron furniture, chandeliers, fine linens, and
large, glazed olive oil jars, pots, and urns.

worn tools and fresh blooms

*Distressed shelves illustrate display
ideas in Avant Garden in Dallas, Texas.
Cut blooms and blooming plants add
color to the mix of planters, stands, clay
pots, and garden accessories.*

Admirers of well-worn finds and
furniture scour the Liberty & Sons Antiques
Market for treasures for their home and
gardens. Early 20th-century pottery, toys,
and textiles add to the treasures.

aged garden-style finds

artifacts *for* inside

Ginger Barber Design Inc., The Sitting Room,
in Houston, Texas, entices shoppers with
real-room settings filled with new and vintage
garden-style furniture and accessories.
Unusually shaped, dried topiaries and glazed,
European pots are part of the mix.

for *dining* alfresco

Garden decorators who entertain on their
terraces find colorful European pottery,
candles, linens, and accessories at Impressions
in fashionable Carmel, California.

casual *elegance* in Carmel

Tancredi & Morgen, in Carmel, is part
of the shopping scene in the picturesque
California coastal town. Shoppers choose
from the artful mix of fragments,
garden ornaments, baskets, and plants.

Alabama

The Elegant Earth
1907 Cahaba Road
Birmingham, Alabama 35223
205/870-3264

Christopher Glenn
2713 19th St. S
Birmingham, Alabama 35209
205/870-1236

Sweet Peas
2829 Linden Ave.
Birmingham, Alabama 35209
205/879-3839

Potager
428 Main Ave.
Northport, Alabama 35476
205/752-4761

Arizona

**The Tended Earth Antique
and Flower Market**
6 Camino Otero
Tubac, Arizona 85646
520/398-2358

**Gift Shop at Tucson Botanical
Gardens**
2150 N. Alvernon Way
Tucson, Arizona 85712
520/326-9686

River Road Nursery
2450 E. River Road
Tucson, Arizona 85718
520/577-6255

Arkansas

Garden Pleasures
128 Spring St.

Eureka Springs, Arkansas 72632
501/253-5858 or 888/428-9594

Grand Finale
1601 Rebsamen Park Road
Little Rock, Arkansas 72202
501/661-9242

California

Bale Mill
3431 St. Helena Hwy. N
St. Helena, California 94574
707/963-4595

Vanderbilt and Company
1429 Main St.
St. Helena, California 94574
707/963-1010

The Mosswood Collection
6550 Washington St.
Yountville, California 94599
707/944-8151

Tivoli
1432 Main St.
St. Helena, California 94574
707/967-9399

Francesca-Victoria
250 Crossroads Blvd.
Carmel, California 93923
408/624-4141; fax: 408/624-1331

The Grove Homescapes
472 Lighthouse Ave.
Pacific Grove, California 93950
831/656-0864

Impressions
114 Crossroads Blvd.
Carmel, California 93923
831/624-9688

Tancredi & Morgen
7174 Carmel Valley Road
Carmel, California 93923
831/625-4477

Devonshire
Ocean Avenue and Monte Verde
P.O. Box AB
Carmel, California 93921
408/626-4601

Nest (on Fillmore)
2300 Fillmore St.
San Francisco, California 94115
415/292-6199; fax: 415/674-1216

Lumbini
156 S. Park St.
San Francisco, California 94107
415/896-2666

Maison D'Etre
5330 College Ave.
Oakland, California 94618
510/658-0698

The Gardener
1836 Fourth St.
Berkeley, California 94710
510/548-4545

Omega Salvage
2407 San Pablo Ave.
Berkeley, California 94702
510/843-7368; fax: 510/843-7123

Omega Salvage
2400 San Pablo Ave.
Berkeley, California 94702
510/843-7368

Omega Too
2204 San Pablo Ave.
Berkeley, California 94702
510/843-3636

Zonal
568 Hayes
San Francisco, California 94102
415/255-9307

Zonal
2139 Polk St.
San Francisco, California 94109
415/563-2220

Swallow Tail
2217 Polk St.
San Francisco, California 94109
415/567-1555

Yard Art
2188 1/2 Sutter St. at Pierce
San Francisco, California 94115
415/346-6002; fax: 415/202-7110

Gordon Bennett
2102 Union St.
San Francisco, California 94123
415/929-1172

Gordon Bennett
900 N. Point
San Francisco, California 94109
415/351-1172

Gordon Bennett
1129 Howard Ave.
Burlingame, California 94010
650/401-3647

Our Own Stuff Gallery Garden
3017 Wheeler St.
Berkeley, California 94705
510/540-8544

Roger's Gardens
2301 San Joaquin Hills Road
Corona Del Mar, California 92625
949/640-5800

Architectural Salvage
1971 India St. Little Italy
San Diego, California 92101
619/696-1313; fax: 619/696-7759

Hooks & Lattice, A Garden Market
3623 India St.
San Diego, California 92103
619/294-7609; 800/896-0978
fax: 619/294-7690

The Cedros Trading Co.
307 S. Cedros
Solano Beach, California 92075
619/794-9016

Argo
111 S. Cedros Ave.
Solana Beach, California 92075
619/793-0410

Austin Morgan
2002 Jimmy Durante Blvd.
Studio 300, The Atelier
Del Mar, California 92014
619/259-4230

Jungle Blue
1555 Camino Del Mar
#308, Del Mar Plaza
Del Mar, California 92014
619/792-9888

French Garden Shoppe
3951 Goldfinch St.
Mission Hills
San Diego, California 92103
619/295-4573

Maison En Provence
820 Fort Stockton Drive
Mission Hills
San Diego, California 92103
619/298-5318

Bazaar Del Mundo
Old Town State Historic Park
2754 Calhoun St., Old Town
San Diego, California 92110
619/296-3161

King and Company
7470 Girard Ave.
LaJolla, California 92037
619/454-1504

Pied a Terre
7645 Girard Ave.
LaJolla, California 92037
619/456-4433

From My Garden
7910 Girard Ave. #8

LaJolla, California 92037
619/456-3961

Retreads Inc. Antique Liquidation Service
3220 Adams Ave.
Normal Heights
San Diego, California 92116
619/284-3999; fax: 619/284-3967

Vintage Rose
324 S. Cedros Ave.
Solana Beach, California 92075
619/792-1668

Paris Flea Market
244 N. Hwy. 101
Encinitas, California 92024
760/633-1373

Magnolia Creek
1057 S. Coast Hwy. 1
Encinitas, California 92024
760/944-7033

Mex-Art Pottery
1155 Morena Blvd.
San Diego, California 92110
619/276-5810

Hortus
284 E. Orange Grove Blvd.

Good Buys In Vintage Garden Furniture And Fragments:

Walnut, Iowa:
A variety of small, locally owned shops sell affordable furniture and architectural fragments. Call 712/784-2100 for information.

Omaha, Nebraska:
Second Chance, 1125 Jackson Street, Omaha, Nebraska 68102 402/346-4930, sells vintage garden furniture at below-shop prices. Look for good buys at the end of the summer.

Essex, Massachusetts:
Over 30 shops, with everything from fine antiques and hand-made pieces to flea market treasures including old garden furniture and tools, are concentrated on or near Maine Street. Call 978/283-1601 for more information.

Woodbury, Connecticut:
In addition to shops specializing in garden ornaments and furnishings, many of the other 35 or so shops in this New England town carry garden pieces. Call the Woodbury Antiques Dealers Association, 203/263-5611, for more information.

New Orleans, Louisiana:
Magazine Street is a mecca for design, fine antique, and second-hand shops. In addition to shops listed in the Louisiana source list, other shops sell vintage garden furniture. and ornaments.

Pasadena, California 91104
626/792-8255
Garden
13365 Ventura Ave.
Sherman Oaks, California 91423
818/788-3400
American Rag
Maison Midi
148 South La Brea
Los Angeles, California 90036
323/935-3157
Demolicious
7912 Melrose Ave.
Los Angeles, California 90046
323/655-6600

Acquisitions
1020 S. Robertson
Los Angeles, California 90035
310/289-0196

Colorado
Devonshire
220 S. Mill St.
Aspen, Colorado 81611
970/925-4820

Connecticut
Michael D. Trapp
7 River Road
West Cornwall, Connecticut 06796
860/672-6098
The Ivy Urn
115 Mason St.
Greenwich, Connecticut 06830
203/661-5287
Devonshire
42 West Putnam Ave.
Greenwich, Connecticut 06830
203/622-0648
Kenneth Lynch & Sons
P.O. Box 488, 84 Danbury Road
Wilton, Connecticut
203/762-8363
Jonathan Peters
P.O. Box 2490
5 Main St.
New Preston, Connecticut 06777
860/868-9017
Garden House
5 Main St.
New Preston, Connecticut 06777
860/868-6790; fax: 860/868-9221
Country Loft Antiques
557 Main St. S
Woodbury, Connecticut 06798
203/266-4500
Eleish-Van Breems Antiques
487 Main St. S
Woodbury, Connecticut 06798
203/263-7030
Wayne Pratt Antiques
346 Main St. S
Woodbury, Connecticut 06798
203/263-5676
Art Pappas Antiques
113 Main St. S
Woodbury, Connecticut 06798
203/266-0374
Rosebush Farm
Corner Rt. 6 & Rt. 317
Woodbury, Connecticut 06798
203/266-9114 or 203/266-9115

Pickets, an English Garden Shop
1894 Bronson Road
Fairfield, Connecticut 06430
203/254-0012

Florida
Adam & Eve Salvage
528 16th St.
West Palm Beach, Florida 33480
561/655-1022
The Brass Scale, Too
3721 S. Dixie Hwy.
West Palm Beach, Florida 33405
561/832-8410

Devonshire
340 Worth Ave.
Palm Beach, Florida 33480
561/833-0796
Devonshire
1290 Third St. S
Naples, Florida 34102
941/643-5888
Apenberry's
407 W. Fairbanks Ave.
Winter Park, Florida 32789
407/644-5909
Artesana
242 W. Garden St.
Pensacola, Florida 32501
850/433-4001
Celebrations the Florist
17 N. 12th Ave.
Pensacola, Florida 32501
850/433-2022
The Gourd Garden and Curiosity Shop
4808 E. County Road 30-A
Santa Rosa Beach, Florida 32459
850/231-2007
Monet Monet
100 E. Scenic Highway 30A
Grayton Beaah, Florida 32459
850/231-5117

Gunby's on the Curve
4415 Scenic 30-A E
Seagrove, Florida 32459
850/231-5958
**Florida Victorian
Architectural Salvage**
112 W. Georgia Ave.
Deland, Florida 32720
904/734-9300; fax: 904/734-1150

Georgia
Ryan Gainey & Co.
2973 Hardman Court NE
Atlanta, Georgia 30305
404/233-2050
Boxwoods Gardens & Gifts
100 E. Andrews Drive
Atlanta, Georgia 30305
404/233-3400
Back to Square One
1054 N. Highland Ave.
Atlanta, Georgia 30306
404/815-9970
Hollyhock
22B E. Andrews Drive
Atlanta, Georgia 30305
404/233-4412
Habersham Gardens
2067 Manchester St.
Atlanta, Georgia 30324
404/873-4702
Lush Life
146 E. Andrews Drive
Atlanta, Georgia 30305
404/841-9661
Dargan Gardens
(custom garden furniture and accessories; by appointment)
2961 Hardman Court
Atlanta, Georgia 30305
404/231-3889;
fax: 404/231-5660
**Pinch of the Past
Architectural Antiques**
109 W. Broughton St.
Savannah, Georgia 31401
912/232-5563
Antiques on the Island
269 Redfern Village
St. Simons Island, Georgia 31522
912/634-1005

Illinois
A New Leaf Studio & Garden
1818 N. Wells St.
Chicago, Illinois 60614
312/642-8553

**Salvage One Architectural
Artifacts**
1524 S. Sangamon St.
Chicago, Illinois 60608
312/733-0098; fax: 312/733-6829
(www.salvageone.com)
Salvage One of Ridgewood
3606 S. Country Club Road
Woodstock, Illinois 60098
815/356-0698; fax: 815/356-6821
(www.salvageone.com)
Jayson's Home & Garden
1885 & 1911 N. Clybourn Ave.
Chicago, Illinois 60614
Home: 773/525-3100
Garden: 773/248-8180
The Urban Gardener
1006 West Armitage Ave.
Chicago, Illinois 60614
773/477-2070; 800-998-7330
Gethsemane Gardens
5809 N. Clark St.
Chicago, Illinois 60626
773/878-5915
Fertile Delta
2760 N. Lincoln Ave.
Chicago, Illinois 60614
773/929-5350
Architectural Artifacts Inc.
4325 N. Ravenswood
Chicago, Illinois 60613
773/348-0622
**Ziggurat Architectural
Ornaments**
1702 N. Milwaukee Ave.
Chicago, Illinois 60647
773/227-6290
The French Look, Inc.
363 W. Erie St.
Chicago, Illinois 60610
312/587-0200; fax: 312/587-0233
Classic Garden Ornaments
83 Longshadow Lane
Ponoma, Illinois 62975
618/893-4831
Crickets
404 South Main St.
Galena, Illinois 61036
815/777-6176; fax: 815/777-6621

**The Urban Gardener's
Countryside**
110 S. Main St.
Galena, Illinois 61036
815/777-0478
**Craig Bergmann's Country
Gardens**
700 Kenosha Road, P.O. Box 424
Wintrop Harbor, Illinois 60096
847/746-0311
Cire' Art de Vivre
226 North Main St.
Galena, Illinois 61036
815/777-8316
Steven Shelton Antiques
314 State St.
Alton, Illinois 62002
618/462-6610

Iowa
The Potting Shed
3141 Hwy. 6 Trail
Homestead, Iowa 52236
319/622-3094
Cross Creek Antiques
101 Williams Blvd. Hwy. 151
Fairfax, Iowa 52228
319/846-8173
Sisters Garden
4859 Hwy. 1 SW
Kalona, Iowa 52247
319/683-2046
**My Sister Shabby's Place on
Fifth**
304 S. Fifth St.
West Des Moines, Iowa 50265
515/255-8022 or 888/SHABBY-4
Sow a Seed
220 Pearl St.
West Hwy. 83
Walnut, Iowa 51577
712/784-3320

Kentucky
Architectural Salvage
618 E. Broadway
Louisville, Kentucky 40202
502/589-0670;
fax: 502/589-4024

shopping:

(Architectural Salvage.com)
**Delaware River Trading
Company**
209 Woodland Ave.
Lexington, Kentucky 40508
800/732-4791

Louisiana
Aux Belles Choses
3912 Magazine St.
New Orleans, Louisiana 70115
504/891-1009
Orient Expressed Imports
3905 Magazine St.
New Orleans, Louisiana 70115

504/899-3060; fax: 504/899-5566
The Bank
2609 Third St.
New Orleans, Louisiana 70113
504/897-5012
American Aquatic Gardens
621 Elysian Fields
New Orleans, Louisiana 70117
504/944-0410
Coles' Florist (two shops)
6060 Jones Creek Road
Baton Rouge, Louisiana 70817
504/751-2233
190 Lee Drive
Baton Rouge, Louisiana 70808
504/751-2233
Aux Vieux Paris Antiques
1040 Henri Penne Road
Breaux Bridge, Louisiana 70517
318/332-2852; fax: 318/332-6053
Aux Vieux Paris Antiques

7219 Perrier St.
New Orleans, Louisiana 70118
504/866-6677; 504/866-8731
gardenArt
109-B Rena Drive
Lafayette, Louisiana 70503
318/237-1005
Antiques and Interiors
616 General Mouton

Lafayette, Louisiana 70501
318/234-4776
Peter Patout Antiques
920 Royal St.
New Orleans, Louisiana 70116
504/522-0582
**New Orleans Auction
Galleries, Inc.**
801 Magazine St.
New Orleans, Louisiana 70130
504/566-1849; fax: 504/566-1851
Bush Antiques
2109 Magazine St.
New Orleans, Louisiana 70130
504/581-3518
The Garden Trellis
8015 Maple St.
New Orleans, Louisiana 70118
504/861-1953
Wirthmore Antiques
3727, 5723, and 3900 Magazine St.
New Orleans, Louisiana 70115
504/269-0660
Just Cherry's
204 Louisiana Ave.
West Monroe, Louisiana 71291
318/397-2418

Maine
Brambles
Main Street
Damariscotta, Maine 04563
207/563-2800
Corey Daniels
2208 Rt. 1 (Post Road)
Wells, Maine 04090
207/646-5301
Riverbank Antiques
1755 Rt. 1 (Post Road)
Wells, Maine 04090
207/646-6314
Art Smith at Wells Union
Rt. 1, 1755 Post Road
Wells, Maine 04090
207/646-6996
Lily's
Main Street, Cornish Village
Cornish, Maine 04020
207/625-2366
Matthew and Helen Robinson
70 Front St.
Bath, Maine 04530
207/443-5856

Maryland
DHS Designs
86 Maryland Ave.

Annapolis, Maryland 21401
410/280-3466
DHS Design
6521 Friel Road
Queenstown, Maryland 21658
410/827-8167
The Well-Furnished Garden
9207 Beech Hill
Bethesda, Maryland 20817
301/469-0268 (by appointment)

Massachusetts
Charles River St. Antiques
45 River St.
Boston, Massachusetts 02114
617/742-9120
R.F. Callahan Antiques
82 Charles St.
Boston, Massachusetts 02114
617/742-3303
Towne and Country Home
99 B Charles St.
Boston, Massachusetts 02114
617/742-9120
Geffner/Schatzky Antiques
40 Main St.
S. Egremont, Massachusetts 01258
413/528-0057
Weeds
14 Centre St., P.O. Box 1403
Nantucket, Massachusetts 02554
508/228-5200
Grass Roots Bloomist
17 Centre St.
Nantucket, Massachusetts 02554
508/228-4450
Devonshire
35 Centre St.
Nantucket, Massachusetts 02554
508/325-8989
Gatherings
27 Dock Square
Rockport, Massachusetts 01966
978/546-5827; fax: 978/546-6655
South Essex Antiques
166 Eastern Ave. (Rt. 133)
Essex, Massachusetts 01929
978/768-6373
Howard's Flying Dragon
136 Main St.
Essex, Massachusetts 01929
978/768-7282
Main Street Antiques
44 Main St.
Essex, Massachusetts 01929
978/768-7039
White Elephant Shop

32 Main St.
Essex, Massachusetts 01929
978/768-6901
Vintage Flowers of Osterville
25 Wianno Ave.

Osterville, Massachusetts 02655
508/428-6089; fax: 508/428-5832

Michigan
Lakeside Depot
14906 Red Arrow Hwy.
Lakeside, Michigan 49116
616/469-9700
Anthony Kavanagh Antiques
101 Generations Drive
Three Oaks, Michigan 49128
616/469-6569
Lovell & Whyte
14950 Lakeside Road
Lakeside, Michigan 49116
616/469-5900
Riviera Gardens
16024 Red Arrow Hwy.
Union Pier, Michigan 49129
616/469-6623; fax: 616/469-6575

Minnesota
Acres
1426 W. 28th St.
Minneapolis, Minnesota 55408
612/872-4122
Bloomsbury Market Inc.
403 S. Cedar Lake Road
Minneapolis, Minnesota 55405
612/377-7636
Casabella
5027 France Ave. S
Edina, Minnesota 55410
612/927-4875; fax: 612/927-5242
**Camrose Hill Flower Studio
and Farm Shop**
210 North Main
Stillwater, Minnesota 55082
612/351-9631

National Retail And Mail-Order Sources

Specialty items

Bryant Clifford Studio (decorative pots, planters, birdhouses)
Fredericksburg, Virginia
540/373-1972

Esperanza Imports
(products include portable outdoor fireplaces)
Tulsa, Oklahoma
800/277-9099

Jackalope
(Southwestern style products, including outdoor fireplaces, retail location)
Santa Fe, New Mexico
800/753-7757

Williams-Sonoma
(table linens, herb baskets, wreaths)
800/541-2233

Panache
(outdoor entertaining)
800/454-6587

Pierre Deux
(retail stores with French-style gardening accessories)
800/774-3773

Chambers
(botanical motif linens)
800/334-9790

Garnet Hill
(botanical motif linens)
800/622-6216)

Ashurst Studios
(botanical prints)
P.O. Box 760
Locust Grove, Virginia 22508
888/332-8922

Aluminum Pottery Co.
(mail-order only, specialty pots and containers)
P.O. Box 269
Devon, Pennsylvania 19333
610/296-8882; 610/296-0201

your
shopping:

Mississippi
Everyday Gardener
2945 Old Canton
Jackson, Mississippi 39216
601/981-0273
Hal Garner Antiques
610-614 Franklin St.
Natchez, Mississippi 39120
601/445-8416

Missouri
The Gifted Gardener
8935 Manchester
St. Louis, Missouri 63144
314/961-1985; fax: 314/961-1859
The Gifted Gardener
5773 Westwood Drive
St. Charles, Missouri 63304
314/498-5560; fax: 314/498-5523
**Missouri Botanical Garden
Gift Shop**
4344 Shaw
St. Louis, Missouri 63110
314/577-5137
Chadfield Garden
2420 Saint Louis Galleria
St. Louis, Missouri 63117
314/725-0197
The Bug Store
113 W. Argonne
Kirkwood, Missouri 63122
314/966-2287
Maries Hollow Herb Farm
32296 Maries Road 213
Vienna, Missouri 65582
573/422-3906
Trapp and Company
4110 Main
Kansas City, Missouri 64111
816/931-6940; fax: 816/931-7389
Christopher Filley
Antiques and Decorative Arts
1721 W. 45th
Kansas City, Missouri 64111
816/561-1124
Grandeur Gardens,
Ltd.
Country Club Plaza
223 W. 47th St.
Kansas City,
Missouri 64112

816/561-2212; fax: 816/561-2217
Smith & Burstert
122 Southwest Blvd.
Kansas City, Missouri 64108
816/531-4772
Antiques and Oddities
1732 Cherry St.
Kansas City, Missouri 64108
816/842-4606

Nebraska
Vago
1120 Jackson St.
Omaha, Nebraska 68102
402/346-3132
Regency Antiques
120 Regency Parkway
Omaha, Nebraska 68114
402/391-7730

New Hampshire
Copperhead North
RR2, Box 294
Colebrook, New Hampshire 03576
603/237-8266

New Jersey
**Delaware River Trading
Company**
15 Trenton Ave.
Frenchtown, New Jersey 08825
800/732-0791
Seibert & Rice
P.O. Box 365
Short Hills, New Jersey 07078
973/467-8266; 973/379-2536
Rising Sun Gardens
7C Chris Court
Dayton, New Jersey 08810
732/274-2059

New York
Treillage
418 E. 75th St.
New York, New York 10021
212/535-2288
Takashimaya
693 Fifth Ave.
New York, New York 10022

212/350-0100
Gray Gardens
461 Broome St.
New York, New York 10013
212/966-7116
Potted Gardens
27 Bedford St.
New York, New York 10014
212/255-4797
Elizabeth Street Gallery
1176 Second Ave.
New York, New York 10021
212/644-6969
Folly
13 White St.
New York, New York 10001
212/925-5861
Lexington Gardens
1011 Lexington Ave.
New York, New York 10021
212/861-4390
Munder Skiles
799 Madison Ave.
New York, New York 10021
212/717-0150
Rooms and Gardens
290 Lafayette St.
New York, New York 10012
212/431-1297
Urban Archaeology
143 Franklin St. (main store)
New York, New York 10013
212/431-4646
Urban Archaeology
285 Lafayette St.
New York, New York 10012
212/431-6969
The Garden Antiquary
724 Fifth Ave. (by appointment)
New York, New York 10021
212/757-3008
The Shop in the Garden
New York Botanical Garden
200th Street and Southern Blvd.
Bronx, New York 10458
718/817-8700
Devonshire
P.O. Box 1860 Main St.
Bridgehampton, New York 11937
516/537-2661

Devonshire
52 Newton Lane
East Hampton, New York 11937
516/329-5392
Hunters & Collectors
Montauk Hwy. at Poxabogue Lane
Bridgehampton, New York 11932
516/537-4233
Urban Archaeology
2231 Montauk Hwy.
Bridgehampton, New York 11932
516/537-0124
Mecox Gardens
257 County Road 39A
Southampton, New York 11968
516/287-5015; fax: 516/287-5018
IvyVine Topiaries Ltd.
Saratoga Springs

New York 12866
518/587-9642
Botanicus Inc.
446 Warren St.
Hudson, New York 12534
518/828-0520
Fern
554 Warren St.
Hudson, New York 10534
518/828-2886
Boards and Beams
137 Poultney St. (Route 4)
Whitehall, New York 12887
518/642-2971
Georgica Creek Antiques
Rt. 27 Montauk Highway
Long Island, New York 11975
516/537-0333

North Carolina
Dovecote Home and Garden Shop
(near Chapel Hill)

2000 Fearrington Village Center
Pittsboro, North Carolina 27312
919/542-1145
Boone's Antiques
2014 Highway 301 S
Wilson, North Carolina 27895
252/237-1508; fax: 252/237-8609
Climbing the Wall
202 S. Columbia St.
Gastonia, North Carolina 28054
704/852-3848
A Proper Garden
2 Ann St.
Wilmington, North Carolina 28401
910/256-0377
Vertu Homes
69 Biltmore Ave.
Asheville, North Carolina 28801
828/253-0099
The Gardener's Cottage
34 All Souls Crescent
Asheville, North Carolina 28803
828/277-2020

Other Sources:

The New York Botanical Garden Spring Show is every April. The nationally known show features garden ornaments and furnishings. For information for the preview party, call 718/817-8557; for show information, call 718/817-8700.

Sotheby's, the auction house, holds an annual auction of antique garden statuary every spring. Call Sotheby's New York general number, 212/606-7000.

The Triple Pier Expo Shows in New York are outstanding sources of architectural salvage and all kinds of garden furnishings and antiques. The shows are held in the spring and fall. For specific dates, contact Stella Show Management Company, 147 West 24th St., New York, New York, 10011; 212/255-0020. Stella also organizes a late winter show, Gramercy Garden Antique Show, at the Gramercy Park Armory in New York City. For information, call 212/255-0020.

The Antiques and Gardens Show of Nashville, Tennessee, is held annually in February. Call 615/352-1282.

For information on spring and summer shows in The Hamptons (Long Island, New York) call 516/537-0333.

The Community House Antiques Show, in March, Birmingham, Michigan features garden antiques. Call 248/644-5832.

The Memphis, Tennessee, Antiques, Garden and Gourmet Show is in February. Call 919/929-0571.

your shopping:

Charlotte's Garden
715 Providence Road
Charlotte, North Carolina 78207
704/333-5353
Lazy Hill Farm Designs
P.O. Box 235
Colerain, North Carolina 27924
252/356-2828
The Stone Lantern
P. O. Box 309, 395 Main St.
Highlands, North Carolina 28741
828/526-2769 or 800/437-2741;
fax: 828/526-4751
Tiger Mountain Woodworks
P.O. Box 1088
2089 Dilliard Road
828/526-5577

Oklahoma
Garden Complements, Inc.
9119 N. Western Ave.
Oklahoma City, Oklahoma 73114
405/810-8512 or 800/886-7775

Pennsylvania
Jon Carloftis
P.O. Box 57
Erwinna, Pennsylvania 18920

610/294-8057; 908/996-7642
Hen-Feathers
250 King Manor Drive
King of Prussia, Pennsylvania
19406-2566
610/277-0800; fax: 610-277-9042
800/282-1910
Monroe Coldren & Son
723 E. Virginia Ave.
West Chester, Pennsylvania 19380
610/692-5651; fax: 610/918-1722

John Burns
Kutztown Used Furniture
21 East Main St.
Kutztown, Pennsylvania 19530
610/683-3441
**Elizabeth Schumacher's
Garden Accents**
4 Union Hill Road
West Conshohocken, Pennsylvania
19428
610/825-5525; fax: 610/825-4817

Rhode Island
Devonshire
302 Thames St.
Newport, Rhode Island 02840
401/846-8210; fax: 401/849-6990

South Carolina
Charleston Gardens
61 Queen St.
Charleston, SC 29401
843/723-0252 or 800/469-0118
(www.charlestongardens.com)
Gates of Charleston
73 Broad St.,
Charleston, South Carolina 29401
843/958-0040

The Houseplant
16 Laurens Road
Greenville, South Carolina 29607
864/242-1589

Tennessee
The Urban Gardener
742 Mount Moriah Road
Memphis, Tennessee 38117
901/374-9964
Gardener's Gallery
921 Barton
Chattanooga, Tennessee 37405
423/265-3170
Garden Park Antiques
515 W. Thompson Lane
Nashville, Tennessee 37211
615/254-1996
Hardy Todd
2207 Jefferson Ave.
Memphis, Tennessee 38104
901/726-1359
Randy Farmer
105 Heady Drive
Nashville, Tennessee 37205
615/354-1267

Texas
Avant Garden
4 Highland Park Shopping Village
Dallas, Texas 75205
214/559-3432
**Liberty & Sons Antiques
Market**
1506 Market Center Blvd.
Dallas, Texas 75207
214/748-3329; fax: 214/748-4447
**Rolston & Bonick Antiques
for the Garden**
2905 N. Henderson
Dallas, Texas 75206
214/826-7775
Utopia Antiques
The Mews
1708 Market Center Blvd.
Dallas, Texas 75207
214/443-9999
Jackson's Lemon Ave. Pottery
6050 Lemon Ave.
Dallas, Texas 75209
214/350-9200
Idle Hours
233 E. Main
Fredericksburg, Texas 78624
830/997-2908
Ginger Barber Design Inc.
The Sitting Room

2402 Quenby St.
Houston, Texas 77005
713/523-1932; fax: 713/523-1929
The Garden Gate
5122 Morningside Dr.
Houston, Texas 77005
713/528-2654; fax: 713/528-0074
**Kay O'Toole Antiques and
Eccentricities**
1921 Westheimer Road
Houston, Texas 77098
713/523-1921
The Gardener's
1209 W. Anderson Lane
Austin, Texas 78757
512/452-2610
Thompson + Hanson
2770 Edloe
Houston, Texas 77027
713/622-6973; fax: 713/626-2317
Gardens
1818 W. 35th St.
Austin, Texas 78703
512/451-5490
Good & Co
248 S. Main
Boerne, Texas 78006
830/249-6101
The Garden Shoppe
2345 Calder
Beaumont, Texas 77702
409/835-3266

Vermont
Simply Vermont
Rt. 2, P.O. Box 175
E. Montpelier, Vermont 05651
888/768-9019

Virginia
Wickets
17 S. Madison St., P.O. Box 1225
Middleburg, Virginia 20118
540/687-5505

The Bittersweet Gardens
6472 Main St.
The Plains, Virginia 20198
540/253-5700
Twig House
132 Maple Ave.
East Vienna, Virginia
703/255-4985
Garden Design
3317 Cary St.
Richmond, Virginia 23221
804/358-8763; fax: 804/358-8829
Terracottage
703 W. Main St.
Charlottesville, Virginia
804/923-3913

Washington, D.C.
Marston Luce
1314 21st St. NW
Washington, D.C. 20036
202/775-9460

Washington
A Garden of Distinction
5819 6th Ave. S
Seattle, Washington 98108
206/763-0517l; fax: 206/762-2002
(gardenpots@aol.com; web site:
agardenofdistinction.com)
Go Outside
111 Morris St.
P.O. Box 216
LaConner, Washington 98257
360/466-4836
Left Bank Antiques
1904 Commercial Ave.
Anacortes, Washington 98221
360/293-3022; fax: 360/299-8888
Wild Side Rustic Furniture
P.O. Box 1958
Port Orchard, Washington 98366
360/895-2276
In and Out of the Garden
16307 115th Ave. SW
Vashon Island, Washington 98070
206/567-5047

Wisconsin
Down to Earth
W. 62, N. 553 Washington Ave.
Cedarburg, Wisconsin 53012
414/375-7060
Monches Farm
5890 Monches Road
Colgate, Wisconsin 53017
414/966-2787

Kohler Gardener
The Shops at Woodlake
765-A Woodlake Road
Kohler, Wisconsin 53044
920/458-5570
Rowe Pottery Works
217 W. Main
Cambridge, Wisconsin 53523
800/356-5003
Rowe Pottery Works
1843 Monroe St.
Madison, Wisconsin 53711
608/256-ROWE

European Shopping

London, England
Deborah Cutler
West Bourne Antiques
Arcade
Portobello Road
London, England
0181-675-4699
The Chelsea Gardener

123-125 Sydney St., Kings
Road
London, England SW3 6NR
0171-352-5656
fax: 0171-352-3301
Clifton's Little Venice
3 Warwick Place
London W9 2PS
0171-289-7894
fax: 0171-286-4215

Paris, France
Forestier
55 Bis Quai de Valmy
Paris, France 75010
42-45-4236
**Jardins
Imaginairies**
5 Rue D'Assas
Paris, France 75006
42-22-8802

Page 8: (Upper left) produced by Sharon Owen Haven; photography by Ed Gohlich, Coronado, California. (Lower left) design: Sharon Mandel and Lorraine Schacht, Lorin Marsh, New York, New York; photography: Bill Holt, Seattle, Washington. (Upper right) design: Sandra Ford, E. Jeannie Merson, and Neva Moskowitz, St. Louis, Missouri; regional editor: Mary Anne Thomson, St. Louis, Missouri; photography by Barbara Martin, St. Louis, Missouri.

Page 9: Produced by Peggy Bowman; photography by Mike Bowman, Indianapolis, Indiana.

Page 10: (Upper left) produced by Bonnie Maharam, New York; photography by Bill Stites, Rowayton, Connecticut. (Lower right) produced by Bonnie Maharam; photography by Bill Stites and King Au, Studio Au, Des Moines, Iowa.

Page 11: Produced by Bonnie Maharam; photography by Bill Holt.

Page 12: (Upper left) photography by Bill Holt. (Lower left) regional editor: Elaine Markoutsas, Chicago, Illinois; photography by Jim Yochum, Sawyer, Michigan/Tuscon, Arizona. (Upper right) regional editor: Estelle Bond Guralnick, Boston, Massachusetts; photography by Eric Roth, Boston, Massachusetts.

Page 13: Produced by Barbara Mundall; photography by Laurie Black, White Salmon, Washington.

Pages 16-19: Design and styling by Ginger Irby, Point Clear, Alabama; photography by Emily Minton, Atlanta, Georgia.

Page 20: Regional editor: Eileen Deymier, Baltimore, Maryland; photography by Eric Roth.

Page 21: Design by Amy Cornell, Upper Marlboro, Maryland; regional editor: Eileen Deymier; photography by Tim Fields, Baltimore, Maryland.

Page 22: (Left) regional editor: Mary Anne Thomson, St. Louis, Missouri; photography by Barbara Martin. (Right) photography by Beth Singer, Detroit, Michigan.

Page 23: (Left) design by Laurie and Phil Stallone, Cottage Style Design Group, Barrington, Illinois; regional editors: Sally Mauer and Hilary Rose, Northbrook, Illinois; photography by Jenifer Jordan, Waxahachie, Texas. (Right) photography by Bill Holt.

Pages 24-25: Photography by Michael Jensen, Seattle, Washington; drapery fabric: Sunbrella, Glen Raven Mills, Glen Raven, North Carolina.

Page 26: Produced by Tracy Skillin and D.J. Carey; photography by Lynn Karlin, Belfast, Maine.

Page 27: Photography by Judy Watts.

Page 28: Design by Sharon Mandel and Lorraine Schacht, Lorin Marsh, New York, New York; regional editor: Bonnie Maharam; photography by Bill Holt.

Page 29: Regional contributor: Cathy Howard; photography by Stephen Cridland, Portland, Oregon.

Pages 30-31: Architectural design: Jack Arnold, Tulsa, Oklahoma; design: Charles Faudree, Tulsa, Oklahoma; regional editor: Nancy Ingram, Tulsa, Oklahoma; photography by Jenifer Jordan.

Page 32: Photography by Jenifer Jordan.

Page 33: (Left) regional editor: Mindy Pantiel, Boulder, Colorado; Photography by Timothy Murphy, Boulder, Colorado. (Right) regional contributor: Ruth Reiter, Atlanta, Georgia; photography by Steven Mays, New York, New York.

Pages 34-35: Design: Ellen Benjamin and Fred Bates, Chicago, Illinois; regional editor: Elaine Markoutsas, Chicago, Illinois; photography by James Yochum.

Pages 36-37: Design: Charles Faudree; regional editor: Nancy Ingram; photography by Gordon Beall, Chevy Chase, Maryland.

Pages 38-39: Field editor: Mindy Pantiel; photography by Timothy Murphy.

Page 40: Garden design: Margaret Willoughby; regional contributor: Cathy Howard; photography by Stephen Cridland.

Page 41: Regional editor: Trish Maharam, Seattle, Washington; photography by Michael Jensen.

Pages 42-43: Produced by Bonnie Maharam; photography by Bill Stites.

Page 44: Regional editor: Elaine Markoutsas; photography by James Yochum.

Page 45: Produced by Bonnie Maharam; photography by Bill Holt.

Pages 46-47: Photography by Laurie Black.

Page 47: Design: Happy Schmaltz; regional contributor: Ruth Reiter; photography by Mary Carolyn Pindar, Atlanta, Georgia.

Pages 48-49: Design and styling: Wade Scherrer, Des Moines, Iowa; photography by Emily Minton; before photography by Greg Scheideman, Studio Au, Des Moines, Iowa; globe lanterns and fan: Pottery Barn; glass urns and tabletop: Pier One Imports.

Pages 50-51: Design and styling: Wade Scherrer; photography by Bill Hopkins, Des Moines, Iowa; before photography by Greg Scheideman; lounge chair with ottoman: Pottery Barn; magnolia print fabric: Waverly (800/423-5881); birdbath: The Home Depot; hanging glass vases: Horchow Home.

Pages 54-55: Design: Tish Schermerhorn, Nashville, Tennessee; regional editor: Nancy Ingram; photography by Jenifer Jordan.

Page 56: (Left) design: Sven Danielson, Oldwich, New Jersey; regional editor: Bonnie Maharam; photography by Bill Holt. (Right) design: Shiden Montgomery, Richardson, Texas; regional editor: Amy Muzzy Malin, Dallas, Texas; photography by Ira Montgomery, Dallas, Texas.

Page 57: (Left) produced by Mona Dworkin; photography by Tony Giammarino, Brooklyn, New York. (Right) design: Sally McCormick, French Country Living, Falls Church, Virginia; regional editor: Eileen Deymier; photography by Andrew Lautman, Washington, D.C.

Pages 58-59: Architects: Pamela Holmes Pospisil and Meryl Kramer; design: Doris LaPorte Associates, Ltd.; regional editor: Bonnie Mahram; photography by Bryan Whitney, New York, New York.

Page 60: Design: Doris LaPorte Associates, Ltd.; regional editor: Bonnie Maharam; photography by Bryan Whitney.

Page 61: Design: Vicki Moran, Oklahoma City, Oklahoma; regional editor: Nancy Ingram; photography by Jenifer Jordan.

Page 62: Design: Vicki Moran; regional editor: Nancy Ingram; photography by Jenifer Jordan.

Page 63: Design: Sharon Mandel and Lorraine Schacht, Lorin Marsh, New York, New York; regional editor: Bonnie Maharam; photography by Bill Holt.

Pages 64-65: Design: Dale Dulancy, Washington, D.C.; regional editor: Eileen Deymier; photography by D. Randolph Foulds; Potomac, Maryland.

Pages 66-67: Design: Marjory Segal, Well Furnished Home and Garden, Bethesda, Maryland; regional editor: Eileen Deymier; photography by Eric Roth.

Page 68-69: Design: Deborah Reinhart, Design Odyssey Ltd., Kenilworth, Illinois; regional editor: Elaine Markoutsas; photography by James Yochum; sources: wallpaper, drapery fabric, trim, lounge chair: Schumacher, New York, New York, (800/332-3384); cane back settee: Nancy Corzine, New York; mirror: William Switzer & Associates Ltd., Vancover, British Columbia, Canada; antique chairs, sisal rug, desk lamp; velvet pillows, throw: Design Odyssey Ltd.; floor lamp: Decorators Walk; mahogany desk: William Switzer & Associates Ltd.; rugs: Minasian Oriental Rug, Evanston, Illinois.

Pages 70-71: Design: Connie Roschlau, Dallas, Texas; photography by Jenifer Jordan.

Pages 72-73: Design: Karen Keysar, LaPlata, Maryland and Amy Cornell Hammond, Upper Marlboro, Maryland; decorative painting: Judy Robinson, Heron Place Design, Waldorf, Maryland; regional editor: Heather Lobdell, Chevy Chase, Maryland; photography by D. Randolph Foulds.

Pages 74-75: Design: Sonja Willman, Terry Sheets, Vicki Dreste, St. Louis, Missouri; regional editor: Mary Anne Thomson; photography by Barbara Martin.

Pages 76-77: Design: Sally Weaver, LaGrange, Illinois; photography by John Bessler, New York, New York.

Page 78: (Left) design: Elizabeth Gibson-Wakeman, Jacobson's on St. Armand Circle, Sarasota, Florida; regional editors: Sally Mauer and Hilary Rose; photography by Jenifer Jordan. (Right) design: Sharon Tjader, Lake Oswego, Oregon; photography by Jon Jensen, San Francisco, California.

Page 79: (Left) produced by Andrea Caughey; photography by Mark Lohman, Los Angeles, California. (Right) design: Charles Riley, New York, New York; photography Studio Au.

Page 80: Design: Landy Gardner Interiors; regional editor: Nancy Ingram; photography by Rick Taylor, Atlanta, Georgia.

Page 81: Design: John Cannon, Chicago, Illinois; regional editors: Sally Mauer and Hilary Rose; photography by Rick Taylor.

Pages 82-83: Design: Mercedes and Kimberly Latham, Locust Valley, New York; regional editor: Bonnie Maharam; photography by Eric Roth.

Pages 84-85: Design and styling: Wade Scherrer; photography by Bill Hopkins; storage cubes: Pottery Barn; terra-cotta globes and miniature conservatories: Bloomsbury Market Inc., Minneapolis, Minnesota; slipcover fabric: Calico Corners (800/213-6366).

Pages 86-87: Design and styling: Wade Scherrer; photography by Bill Hopkins; slipcover: Pottery Barn; framed print and wall paint: K Mart; finials and lamp: SteinMart.

Pages 88-89: Design and styling: Wade Scherrer; photography by Bill Hopkins; wallpaper (matching fabric available): Seabrook, Memphis, Tennessee (800/238-9152); curtains: K Mart; pottery: Pottery Barn.

Pages 90-91: Design: Missy Connolly, Fern Hill Design, Butler, Maryland; regional editor: Eileen Deymier; photography by Ross Chapple, Waterford, Virginia.

Pages 92-93: Design: Carole Cillino Interiors, Westerly, Rhode Island; regional editor: Estelle Bond Guralnick; photography by Eric Roth.

Page 94: Design: Well Furnished Home and Garden, Bethesda, Maryland; regional editor: Eileen Deymier; photography by Eric Roth.

Page 95: Produced by Mary Anne Thomson; photography by Bryan Whitney.

Pages 96-97: Architect: Jack Arnold; Design: Charles Faudree; regional editor: Nancy Ingram; photography by Jenifer Jordan.

Page 98-99: Architect: Tom Crosby; regional contributor: Ruth Reiter; photography by Laurie Black.

Page 99: Design: Paula Olsson, Pacific Grove, California; photography by Stephen Cridland.

Pages 100-101: Design: Gary Roeberg, Philadelphia, Pennsylvania; regional editor: Eileen Deymier; photography by Tim Fields, Baltimore, Maryland.

Page 102: Design: Mario Buatta, New York, New York; photography by Bill Holt.

Page 103: Design: Angela Wicka, Casabella, Minneapolis, Minnesota; regional editor: Tangi Schaapveld; photography by Susan Gilmore, Minneapolis, Minnesota.

Pages 104-105: Design: Anita L. Philipsborn, Philipsborn Designs Inc., Evanston, Illinois; regional editor: Elaine Markoutsas; sources: wicker settee: Collected Works, Wilmette, Illinois; fabric: Cowtan & Tout, New York, New York, (212/753-4488); sisal rug and curtains: Pottery Barn; terrarium: Anthropologie.

Pages 106-109: Design: Peg Van Dyne, Oklahoma City, Oklahoma; regional editor: Nancy Ingram; photography by Jenifer Jordan.

Pages 110-111: Design: Gretchen Rhodes, Quinn Interiors, Fairfax, Virginia; regional editor: Heather Lobdell; photography by D. Randolph Foulds.

Pages 112-113: Design: Jackie Stoneman, Dallas, Texas; regional editor: Mary Baskin, Waco, Texas; photography by Jenifer Jordan.

Pages 114-115: Produced by Joetta Moulden; photography by Mark Lohman.

Pages 116-117: Design: Peg Gildersleeve; stencil art: Deborah Brackman Design, Nicasio, California; regional editor: Helen Heitkamp; photography by John Vaughan, San Francisco, California.

Page 118: (Left) design: Peg Dobroth, Marblehead Neck, Massachusetts; regional editor: Estelle Bond Guralnick; photography by D. Randolph Foulds. (Right) regional editor: Estelle Bond Guralnick; photography by Eric Roth.

Page 119: (Left) regional editor: Bonnie Maharam; photography by Bill Holt. (Right) produced by Joseph Boehm and Peggy Fisher; photography by Judith Watts.

Page 120: Produced by Tracy Skillin and D.J. Carey; photography by Lynn Karlin.

Page 121: Regional editor: Andrea Caughey; photography by Ed Gohlich.

Pages 122-123: Design: Janis Ribbetrop, Vienna, Virginia; photography by Gordon Beall.

Pages 124-125: Design: Alessandra Branca, Chicago, Illinois; regional editors: Sally Mauer and Hilary Rose; photography by Jenifer Jordan.

Pages 126-127: Design: Susan Tolbert, Atlanta, Georgia; decorative painting: Brian Carter, Atlanta, Georgia; photography by Emily Minton.

Pages 130-139: Design: Elvin McDonald, West Des Moines, Iowa; styling: Wade Scherrer; photography by Emily Minton.

Pages 140-151: Design: Charlotte Comer, Dallas, Texas; regional editor: Mary Baskin; photography by Jenifer Jordan.

Pages 152-159: Design: Ryan Gainey, Atlanta, Georgia; regional editor: Elle Roper, Atlanta, Georgia; photography by Emily Minton. sources: lanterns on skirted table and plates on skirted and patio tables designed and painted by Bob Francisco for The Ryan Gainey Collection (see shop listings); dining room: lamp, cabinet, and frame by Huckleberry Starnea.

Pages 160-169: Design: Gail Miller, Carmel, California; regional editor: Kristine Carber; Menlo Park, California; photography by Jamie Hadley, San Francisco, California.

Pages 170-179: Design: Michael Trapp, West Cornwall, Connecticut; regional editor: Elle Roper; photography by Emily Minton.

Pages 182-183 Regional editor: Elle Roper; photography by Emily Minton.

Page 184: Regional editor: Heather Lobdell; photography by Gordon Beall.

Pages 185-187: Regional editor: Elle Roper; photography by Emily Minton.

Pages 188-192: Photography by Emily Minton.

Pages 195: Regional editor: Heather Lobdell; photography by Gordon Beall.

Pages 196-197: Regional editor: Tangi Schaapveld; photography by Susan Gilmore.

Page 198: Regional Editor: Susan Andrews, Kansas City, Missouri; photography by Roy Inman, Kansas City, Missouri.

Page 198-199 (Middle): field editor: Elaine Markoutsas; photography by James Yochum.

Page 199: Regional editor: Susan Andrews; photography by Roy Inman.

Pages 200-201: Regional editor: Tangi Schvaaveld; photography by Susan Gilmore.

Pages 202-203: Field editor: Elaine Markoutsas; photography by James Yochum.

Pages 204-205: Field editor: Kristine Carber; photography by Jamie Hadley.

Page 206: Regional editor: Joetta Moulden; photography by Fran Brennan.

Page 207: Regional editor: Mary Baskin; photography by Jenifer Jordan.

Page 208: Regional editor: Joetta Moulden; photography by Fran Brennan.

Pages 208-209 (Middle photograph): regional editor: Mary Baskin; photography by Jenifer Jordan.

Page 209: Regional editor: Joetta Moulden; photography by Fran Brennan.

Pages 210-219: Large background photographs by John Reed Forsman, Minneapolis, Minnesota.

the index

the index